Nedda C. Anders

APPLIQUÉ
Old and New

INCLUDING

PATCHWORK AND EMBROIDERY

DOVER PUBLICATIONS, INC.

New York

Frontispiece. A mid-nineteenth century English coverlet shows applied motifs of printed cottons on a white cotton ground. *Victoria and Albert Museum.*

Published in Canada by General Publishing Company, Ltd., 30 Lesmill Road, Don Mills, Toronto, Canada.
Published in the United Kingdom by Constable and Company, Ltd., 10 Orange Street London WC 2.

This Dover edition, first published in 1976, is an unabridged republication of the work first published in 1967, to which has been added one new section (page 72). This edition is published by special arrangement with Hearthside Press, Inc., Publishers, 445 Northern Boulevard, Great Neck, New York 11021, publishers of the original edition. Figures 4–10 were drawn by Bucky King.

International Standard Book Number: 0-486-23246-8
Library of Congress Catalog Card Number: 75-19756

Manufactured in the United States of America
Dover Publications, Inc.
180 Varick Street
New York, N.Y. 10014

To Richard Ian Anders
who designed some
of my favorite appliqués

Acknowledgements

Bucky King, author of *Creative Canvas Embroidery* and co-author (with Lillian S. Freehof) of *Embroideries and Fabrics for Synagogue and Home* has been a generous and wise adviser not only on drawings (many of which she supplied), but also on photographs and text. I deeply appreciate her enthusiasm and counsel.

Also, I am grateful to the talented designers whose work is represented here, and to the staff of arts and crafts museums who quickly, intelligently (and usually anonymously) helped me to find photographs of appliqués for this publication.

Table of Contents

1 *Materials and Design Techniques*

Appliqué, a handsome and unusually decorative form of needlework, has been practiced since ancient times. An example of appliqué on an Egyptian funeral tent preserved in a Cairo museum dates back almost three thousand years. It is, basically, a method of embroidery in which the design is cut out of one material, laid-on and secured to another background material, with stitches around the cut edges. Closely allied to laid-on or onlaid appliqué, as it is now called, is inlaid work, which is appliqué in reverse. In this form of appliqué, the overlaid fabric is cut away to reveal the pattern beneath.

Since the applied material may be cut from oddments of fabric, and often takes the place of what would otherwise be needlework—indeed, at one time it was used as a substitute for tapestry (Plate 1)—appliqué may be called "poor man's embroidery." Even a beginner can easily learn the techniques for achieving lovely and graceful designs on large articles. However, onlaid and inlaid appliqué are also a challenge to the most sophisticated needleworker, because they offer so many opportunities to exercise originality. For example, many different materials, from tiny shells to scraps of fur, can be applied for textural enrichment. Furthermore, embroidery stitches of every complexity can be used to join the appliqué to the ground or to fill in decorative details. Versatile, challenging, giving scope for personal expressiveness, per-

1. A substitute for costly tapestry, this fifteenth century hanging treats the Tristram legend more or less in the manner of German tapestry of that period. It is cloth applied work with design elements outlined in cord. *Victoria and Albert Museum.*

2. A detail of Plate 1, upper right corner.

haps few types of needlework have so broad a range of appeal as appliqué.

You do not need a great many materials for appliqué, but the few you do use should be of the best quality. Complex techniques and elaborate stitchery are not required either, since most of the effect is achieved by superimposing pieces of materials, cut to form shapes or scenes, on a background. Yet you will find this one of the most fascinating kinds of needlework. Although your own individuality can and should be expressed in your work, the following sections will help you get started.

Materials

Embroidery threads

Be sure they are colorfast. Choose threads that relate to the fabric you are using in kind and weight: mercerized and cotton threads for cotton, chintz and linen; silk and silk synthetics on silks, velvets, linens, etc. Thickness of thread should vary—a six-strand thread is good for lightweight fabrics and all-purpose use. Embroidery wools and high-sheen threads are also used for special effects.

Needles

Embroidery needles are good for fine and medium weight threads and fabrics, chenille needles for heavier threads and fabrics. Good pins are also useful.

Scissors

Sharp scissors with pointed blades which close perfectly are essential.

Thimble

You will need one to protect your middle finger when pushing the needle through the fabric.

Fabric for the appliqué

Any material which does not fray easily when cut can be used for appliqué or inlay. Chintz, brocade, linen, velvet, silk, cotton, felt,

3. In the hands of the creative needleworker, scraps of material are the beginning of appliqué. Gisella Loeffler writes: "Inspiration for this stitchery came from the primitive markets of La Paz, Bolivia. Here the Indians spin yarns hand-dyed in brilliant colors — magenta, purple, lemon yellow, turquoise and orange. As I did not carry my painting materials, I got bits of yarn and hand-woven scraps and began my first stitchery." *Gisella Loeffler.*

leather, designs cut from decorator prints—all are good. Be sure that the applied pieces go the same way as the background, otherwise some of the laid-on pieces may pucker. This is particularly important with wall hangings which are usually stretched and mounted. Designs on printed fabric may be cut out and used in appliqué, just as printed papers would be in découpage work. If thin lines of stems, etc. cannot be cut out of the print, they can be added with embroidery stitches.

Today's needleworker can find so many fascinating materials to use for appliqué! Hand-woven fabric, a scrap of crochet, and knitting wool left from afghans and socks supply exciting new textures. So too do furs, feathers, nail heads, pearls, beads, sequins, even tiny pieces of mirror. The chapter on modern appliqué shows many creative uses for such materials. Nylon and some of the other contemporary synthetics have an unfortunate tendency to pucker, however, and should be tested before use.

Fabric for the background

Linen, cottons of all types, chintz, canvas, duckcloth, felt, sailcloth, velvet, satin, silk, damask and plush all are practical because they are firm and leave a clean edge when cut. For lingerie and dainty dress and home appointments, net, organdy, silk and ninon give delicate effects. It is not necessary, or even desirable, that the materials for the ground match those used for the appliqué, but if the finished article is to be washable, it is best that they do. Materials with different tension qualities should not be combined. Organdy, for example, slides and pulls in a quite different way from velvet or plush.

4. "Make me over in the morning from the rag bag of the world" — Bliss Carmen's *Spring Song* might have inspired just such needlework. It pictures two children caught in a spring shower, one wearing a coat of printed percale and carrying an orange linen umbrella, the other wearing a gold slicker and green felt trousers. The sky is pale bluish gray organza; the rocks are light gray corduroy giving the effect of striations; the background is medium gray cotton homespun. Trees are gray fabric light to dark bluish — cotton, woven flannel, and corduroy.

To a discerning eye, the rag bag of scraps and home-brought stuffs has become a rich treasure for needlework art. *J. H. Koslan Schwartz.*

Handling delicate fabrics

Materials that are fragile or fray easily when cut are difficult to manipulate. They can be used if backed as follows: Spread fast-drying paste onto muslin or fine tissue paper. Smooth out and pick off any lumps of paste. Fit the appliqué fabric gently onto the paste and smooth it quickly to expel any air bubbles. Cover the pasted fabrics with clean paper or cloth, and weight it down with heavy objects until it is dry and pressed flat.

Another way to treat materials which fray easily: Spread paste lightly over the cut edges on the reverse side and along the edges only. Mask the edges when the appliqué is laid on the ground material with cord, braid, thread, or by turning in the margins and blind stitching.

If you spread too much paste along the edges of the design, you will find it troublesome to pass the needle through when stitching the appliqué, so be sure to use only a light coating.

Embroidery frames

Most appliqué can be done in the hands, but for large articles like bedspreads and draperies, and those with a great deal of detail embroidery, it may help to have the material stretched on a frame. Keep the frame slack until all the applied pieces are sewn in place, then tighten the frame and do the outline work.

The simplest kind is the hand frame consisting of two wooden hoops. The section on which you are working is placed over the smaller hoop, and the larger hoop is pressed down over the fabric to keep it from puckering. Many appliqué designs can be worked in the hand.

Washing Embroidery

This is possible only if you have used washable materials of the same texture and tension. Wash by squeezing gently, rinse thoroughly in warm water, squeeze by hand and remove excess moisture by rolling in a towel. Do this, using a dry towel, until embroidery is half dry, about ten minutes, then press lightly to avoid flattening the stitches.

If it is necessary to iron the appliquéd pieces, do so on the reverse side, lifting the iron to press each appliqué separately, not by pushing the iron along. If you have to contend with different surface qualities in the applied fabric, work slowly and as the Quaker saying goes, "proceed as the way opens."

Transferring Designs

You can draw your own designs from nature, or copy them from other articles. You can trace pennies, dimes and nickels, triangles, squares and other geometrical shapes. You can trace cooky cutters, barbecue tools, leaves and garden implements as motifs to decorate gift aprons for hostesses, gardeners and outdoor chefs. You can build a reference library of bold shapes suitable for appliqué and have them reduced or enlarged mechanically to the exact size you want (a photostat service for doing this should be listed in the classified telephone directory). And of course you can buy embroidery transfers from needlework shops.

There are several popular methods for getting the design onto the material. You can draw the shapes on the appliqué fabric free hand, then cut them out with sharp scissors. You can use the pounce method, transfer pencils and ink, or tissue paper transfers. If you are using transparent fabric, you can lay the fabric on top of the design to be copied, secure it with pins, then trace it on the fabric using a medium pencil.

Pounce Method

The object is to make a perforated pattern of your design, which you do as follows:

1. Draw the design and trace it onto tracing paper. Place the tracing paper right side up on thick newspaper or folded blanket or ironing board. Using a needle or fine pointed pin stuck in a cork for easy handling, prick out the outline of the design, making clean holes close together (about 10 to an inch).

2. Put this perforated pattern on top of the well-pressed ground fabric. Pin pattern firmly to fabric. Have ready some gray pounce powder in a small saucer. (Pounce powder can be bought or made from equal amounts of white chalk and black charcoal rubbed on fine sandpaper. Gray will show up on white, black or colored fabrics.) Also have ready a pounce pad: Roll tightly a small strip of flannel or felt; stitch it to make it firm, flat and solid. Dip the end of the pounce pad into the pounce powder, shake off surplus powder, then dab the powder through the perforations until all of the design has been treated.

3. Carefully remove the tracing paper and label and store it for future use since it can be used time and again. Lightly blow off any surplus powder, but do not disturb the powder outlining the design.

Fig. 1. Three steps in the pounce method: (a) pricking out the outline; (b) dabbing the powder through the perforations; (c) connecting the dotted lines.

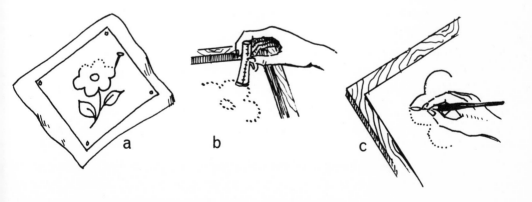

a   b   c

Fig. 2. Pounce method of transferring designs requires chalk, charcoal, sandpaper, pad, paints, brush.

4. Using a thin watercolor and a fine paintbrush, connect the dotted lines to form the design. When dry, the ground fabric is ready to receive the appliqué.

5. Follow the same method of transferring the design to the appliqué fabric, making certain that the threads run in the same direction. Work on the wrong side of the appliqué, reversing the pattern for this purpose, so that the face of the appliqué fabric will not be marked with pounce powder. Cut out the appliqué and number the individual elements on the ground fabric as well as on the appliqué if the design is a complicated one. Stitchery, braid, cord, etc. will cover the markings on the ground fabric. If you are using blind appliqué (see page 33) be sure to allow an extra margin around the design before cutting out the appliqué.

Putting Designs onto Transparent Fabrics

When working with organdy, nylon, silk, or other fine fabrics of this kind, pin the design onto a drawing board or other surface, pin the fabric on top. Be sure that the lines of the design are keyed to the lines of the fabric. Trace the design onto the fabric with a hard pencil.

Putting Designs onto Coarse Fabrics

It is difficult to trace the design onto velvets, knits or coarse or heavily textured fabrics. In this case, use the tacking method. Trace the drawing onto tracing paper, baste the paper in position on the fabric, then carefully make fine tack stitches through both the paper and material, in this way carefully marking all the lines of the design. Tear away the paper and you will find the design left in stitches to be covered by the appliqué.

Dressmaker's Carbon Paper

This makes a simple method of transferring your own design onto fabric. Place the carbon paper face down on the fabric. Lay a tracing of the design on top. Draw the design using a light touch and trying not to rest your hand on it. Draw over all the lines with a sharply pointed pencil or knitting needle. Remove design and carbon paper. The permanent line left by the tracing can be concealed with stitchery, edging, etc. Again, this tracing can be applied to the ground fabric as well as to the appliqué in reverse.

If you do not have dressmaker's carbon paper, find some carbon paper which has been so well used that very little carbon is left on it. Or rub off most of the carbon from new carbon paper with a wad of tissue paper.

Embroidery Transfers

Creative needleworkers discourage the use of bought transfers, but beginners find it a quick and easy method of transferring designs to fabric. The transfer sheet has its design outlined on thin paper. Lay the printed side next to the material, pin into place and, using a moder-

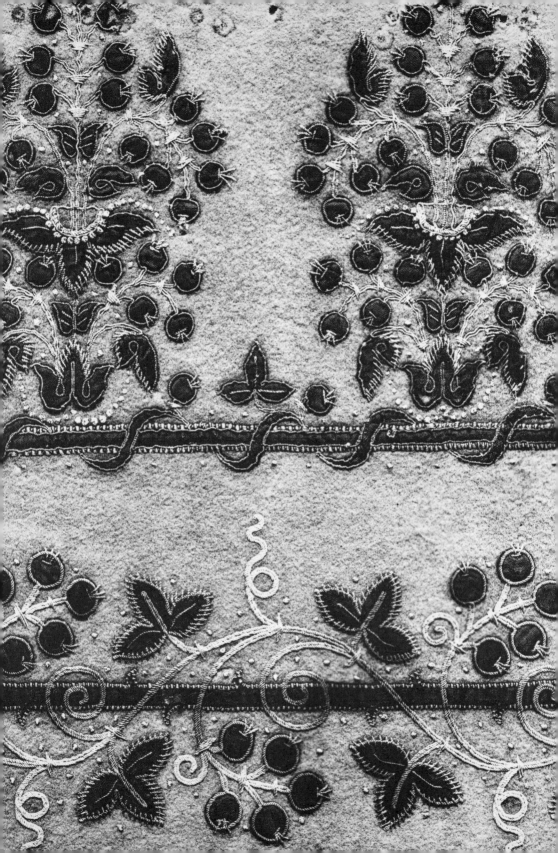

5. A section of a bed hanging — English early seventeenth century — is of black velvet applied to red cloth with yellow cord couched work used for the outlines and details. *Victoria and Albert Museum.*

ately hot iron, apply it to the back. Lift the iron from place to place; do not push it. The heat will melt the outline onto the fabric, leaving a clear design.

Make Your Own Transfer Patterns

You will need a homemade substitute for transfer ink. Dissolve a little sugar in water, then add old-fashioned "laundry blue" for color. Lay tissue paper over the design and trace it through, then trace on the back, so the design irons off the right way. Paint the outlines onto the tissue with a fine paintbrush. Let dry thoroughly before transferring with moderately hot iron. For materials which fray easily, make two transfer patterns—one for ironing onto the background and one to be cut up and transferred to the appliqué.

Color in Appliqué

Appliqué is often done in bold colors with the laid-on fabric strongly contrasted in hue to its background. However, any desired color effect may be achieved. Monochromatic schemes, for example shell pink to deep pink in a luncheon cloth or for a spread for a girl's bed, can be very effective if the applied material makes a strong, clear silhouette against the background. Textural contrast can be provided through stitchery or by other ornamentation, including beads and braids. Analogous colors are very effective in establishing a mood or sense of season. For example, trees and flowers worked in clear yellows and greens will give a predominantly springlike feeling. In dull reds and somber greens the effect would be wintry.

Whatever the combination, however, remember that the fabric which dominates by covering the largest area is usually best in a light, grayed or neutral tone. The secondary, relief or contrast color should be keyed to the dominant color. If the dominant color is a pale cream with a suggestion of pink, and blue is the secondary color, select a blue which has pinkish tones. Small accents can be done in brilliant, intense colors, also keyed to the dominant color — a sharp clear red, a vivid orange, etc. Distribute these color accents throughout the design in some rhythmic and meaningful pattern, not spottily.

Design Principles

Unity, balance, scale, proportion, contrast and rhythm—these are qualities which are fundamental to art. The fundamentals may be expressed in varied ways. For example, ancient Greece had an ideal of beauty based on symmetry; Japan, where aesthetics is a religion, finds perfection in asymmetry. But no matter how tastes change from country to country or from century to century, the fundamentals themselves are constant and immutable.

Unity is more or less easily achieved in most forms of embroidery, because there is something about even the least skilled stitchery which brings all parts of a work into harmony. But in appliqué, the bits and pieces of fabric do not in themselves have a design relationship, and homogeneity must be provided in one of several different ways: (1) by the use of congruous forms and textures, (2) by interlocking or overlapping, (3) by the repetitive element of bold stitchery, (4) by establishing a strong contour line or silhouette of patches against ground fabric and (5) by the use of well-placed color accents.

Balance, another fundamental of design, may also be achieved in different ways. Formal balance requires the use of a central axis, with identical or similar elements of equal visual weight, repeated on each side of the axis, as in Plates 6, 7. Designs of a classical nature al-

6. This example of Resht work (named for a Persian town in which appliqué flourished as a peasant art during the late eighteenth and early nineteenth century) shows cloth patches with details and outlines in silk chain stitch and couched work. *Victoria and Albert Museum.*

most invariably use symmetrical balance. Asymmetrical balance is
less static, less formal, and it is achieved through placement, rather
than by duplication, of units. For example, a large shape placed close
to a central axis will balance a smaller shape placed further way.
Balance is somewhat instinctual; you can prove this by observing two
children on a seesaw. The smaller child will automatically move to
the edge of the board to balance the heavier partner who moves closer
to the center.

Scale and proportion, which deal with size relationships, are the
crucial factors in fabric pictures but some designers hold the mistaken
idea that all the elements in a scene must have the same ratio to each
other as they would in nature. Note, however, that in Plate 8 the fruit

7. *(Opposite)* Another example of Resht work, this prayer rug has cloth
patches with outlines and details in silk chain stitch, and couched work.
Victoria and Albert Museum.

8. A long cushion cover finished off with tassels shows silk and silver thread
on linen canvas, appliqué on white satin, tent and cross stitches, and
couching. *Victoria and Albert Museum.*

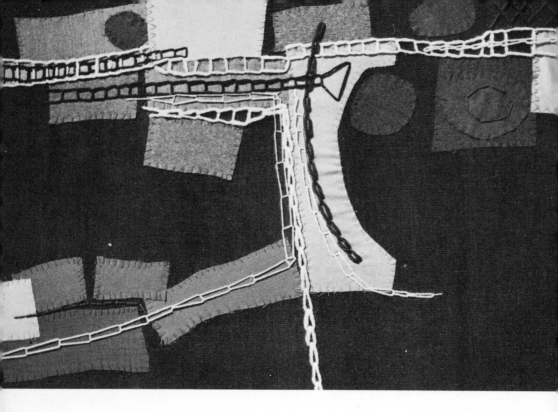

is larger than life, the roots are small in proportion to the trees, but all of them are readily identifiable, and help to support a design concept. Perspective is also influenced by size. Objects which diminish in size and simultaneously are greyed in tone add a feeling of distance, just as in nature distant objects become smaller and less chromatic.

Contrast is the spice of design and must exist in every type of needlework. It can be achieved with varied forms, stitchery with subtle or strong color variation, and with different textures.

Rhythm is created with colors, textures, voids, and their placement in the design, but the most compelling of all the elements is line. Strong heavy lines produce a slow, majestic rhythm; twiggy little lines, as in a Dufy painting, result in a lively rhythm; arcs and ovals are feminine; circles are maternal.

9. *(Opposite)* Here the strong T-shaped contour is a unifying factor, as is the stitchery carried from patch to patch and also to ground fabric. "Study in Blue," a monochromatic work by David Van Dommelen, achieves necessary contrast through tonal variations (light, middle through dark values of blue) and variety in shapes.

10. Embroidery is the strongly unifying element in "Sea Dragon," a handsome example of onlay appliqué in which many layers of organdy are couched to the ground fabric in long and short stitch. *Bucky King.*

Assembling Appliqué and Ground Fabrics

Hand Method 1

For materials which fray easily you will need two sets of the same design, one for the background fabric and one to be cut up and transferred to the applied fabric. Cut out the pieces for the appliqué, leaving a rough margin. Tack the appliqué pieces in place, then buttonhole stitch them carefully, using a close stitch. When the edging is done, cut the extra material neatly away, right up to the purl edge of the buttonholing. You will need sharp, finely pointed scissors. After the cutting out is completed, detail work may be embroidered on.

Hand Method 2

As each piece of appliqué is cut out, lay it exactly over the corresponding shape on the background material. Pin the appliqué into place, being certain to keep it perfectly flat and unwrinkled. If you are work-

11. Cord outlines on linen and green satin in a Spanish pilaster hanging from the late sixteenth century; the outlining helped to flatten the pieces making up the lace-like patterns introduced about this time. *Victoria and Albert Museum.*

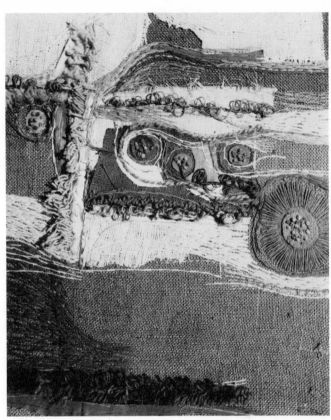

12. *(Left)* Harmony in materials, relationship of textures and contrast of shapes and colors make a pleasing design of an owl. The stitches are spider web, satin, long and short, and cretan. *Mrs. Hans Rudolph. (Photograph by Dick Alcorn.)*

13. *(Right)* In "Flowering Vine," white burlap and colored wools are stitched on mauve burlap with threads ranging from fine to heavy wool rug yarn. Hooking, couching, and French knots are used along with simple line stitches to build up warm, richly complex textural surfaces. *Nancy Belfer.*

ing with large appliqués and are having trouble holding them down flat, put a *thin* coating of paste over the center of the background only before laying down the appliqué. When everything is in place, stitch the applied fabric neatly.

Machine Assemblage

This is described on page 51.

Overlapping of Design Units

When overlapping occurs, leave a ¼-inch margin on the underpiece. If the pieces are to be oversewn at the edge, about 1/16 inch should be left beyond the outline.

In all appliqué, the pieces that are underneath should be completed first so there is a neat, unbroken line at top.

Finishing Touches

The applied fabrics can be held to the background with embroidery stitches, which are also used for filling in details, or with blind appliqué. However, designs in which some edges are embroidered and some blind-appliquéd are the most interesting and varied.

In traditional work the margins are finished with stitching threads of contrasting or matching colors. The thickness of the thread should be related to the thickness of the material: synthetic silk threads for silk, rayon, velvet and linen; mercerized and cotton threads for cottons, chintzes, etc. Embroidery wools are also used to make bold designs which are striking from a distance. These wools also create a special effect, for example, fur in animals or feathers in birds.

Cords, braids of varied widths, hanks of wool, scalloping and other needle-made edgings are used for outlining the appliqué. This edging serves not only to keep the pieces flat, but also, when a contrasting color is used, to define the pattern. Metallic threads are particularly appropriate for church work. If a twisted cord or braid is applied as an edging, it is usually sewn invisibly to the ground fabric. The best way to do this is to separate the strands slightly, then insert the needle between the strands.

If couching is used, see that the laid thread is thick enough to cover and protect the edges. Several thicknesses of a moderate thread laid side by side give a much neater and flatter finish than a single very thick thread. Embroidery wool used double and rug wools are also excellent for this purpose.

Fringes and tassels often decorate the finished article (Plate 14).

14. Appliqué has often been combined with other forms of needle art. In this long cushion cover from sixteenth century Elizabethan England, motifs of linen canvas embroidery worked separately with silk, silver, and silver gilt thread have been laid on black velvet. Tent stitches, with laid work, couching stem and cross stitches were used. *Victoria and Albert Museum.*

2 *Appliqué Types and Methods*

Appliqué may be divided into two broad groups—onlay and inlay—but there are many variations within these groups and many more may be invented by the creative needleworker. Blind appliqué, raised or padded appliqué and iron-on or patching appliqué are just a few discussed in this chapter and illustrated with finished examples. It is not unusual for several forms of needlework to be combined. Plate 14 shows canvas work as part of appliqué. Plate 22 illustrates a combination of bead and bullion appliqué.

Onlay

Blind Appliqué

As this is the quickest and easiest kind of needlework, it is suited to large articles and to designs which utilize patterned materials, in which the charm of ornamental stitchery would be lost. In this kind of appliqué, the applied fabric is secured to the background with a stab or blind hemstitch. Here are the steps:

1. Cut out each piece of material for the appliqué allowing for a narrow turning. This turning will vary with the thickness of the fabric —an allowance of ⅓″ will be enough for most lightweight fabrics.

2. Pin or tack into position, not too close to the edges.

3. Working with sewing cotton in a matching shade, take small regular stitches all around, tucking the extra turning under with the point of the needle as you work.

4. Press very carefully when finished, otherwise there will be bumps around the edges which have been tucked under.

Stitches for Blind Appliqué

Plain Hemming

First crease and fold under the narrow turning on the appliqué piece. Pin in place. Using same color thread as fabric, take a few running stitches on the back of the fabric to secure the thread. Hold in place with regular hem stitches.

Blind Hemming

First crease and fold under the narrow turning. Pin in place. Using same color thread as ground fabric, take a few running stitches to secure the thread to the back of the appliqué fabric. Now take a tiny stitch on the ground fabric. Next pick up a tiny stitch of the folded-under turning, close to the creased edge but still under it. Pass the needle inside the hem for about $\frac{1}{2}$ inch and repeat with another tiny stitch into the ground fabric. Follow with a tiny stitch into the creased turning. Repeat until piece is secured. Do not pull stitches tight.

Stab Hemming

Crease and fold under the narrow turning. Pin in place. Select a thread which matches the fabric to be applied. Secure thread with a few running stitches under the appliqué. Bring the needle through the ground fabric only, but directly under the edge of the appliqué. Make a tiny stitch into the edge of the creased turning, through the appliqué and ground fabric. Bring the needle up $\frac{1}{2}$ inch beyond this stitch and repeat until the piece is secured. The stitches should be so small that they are almost invisible.

15. **Examples of free machine stitchery here are the linen and organdy table cloth, the chair pads of velvet ribbons on linen, and the wall hanging of canvas, also on a linen ground. Designed by Bucky King for an A. I. D. show in Pittsburgh, Pennsylvania.** *(Photograph by Robert W. Franz.)*

16. *(Opposite)* "The Yum Yum Tree" — appliqué and surface stitchery in wool with wool felt leaves applied with cretan stitch; buds in padded detached buttonhole similar to "stump work." *Bucky King.*

Raised or Padded Appliqué

To build up the appliqué, you can cut out cotton, wool or foam batting and insert it under the appliqué. Cut-up strips of nylon stocking can also be used. Push the batting into the corners using a knitting needle, skewer, etc. Outline stitching may be done by hand or machine (Plate 16). You can also raise the appliqué by using stitches as the foundation, adding stitchery to the desired height. Another method is to cut out felt in the desired shape. Make several cut-outs of the shape but decrease them in size. Sew the smallest piece down first, add the next size, stitch all around and then finish with the largest size, which should slope on all sides and make a mound raised in the middle.

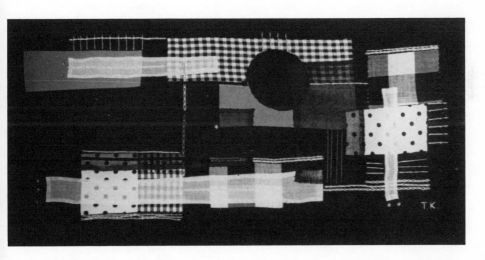

17. Example of blind hemming with emphasis on strong riot pattern in materials. *Tina Krythe.*

Floral Appliqué

Flowers have been favored themes for embroidery through the ages (Plates 18, 19, 20). They are still appealing themes. The flowers can be cut separately using various materials. Then each unit can be tacked into place (the lowest layer first, of course) on the ground fabric. Outlines and flower centers can be worked in various stitches. A floral pillow project is given in the next chapter.

Another type of design with flowers is called Sabrina work. This is appliqué in which brightly colored fabrics are cut into whole designs of fruits, florals, etc. in an all-over motif. The appliqué is then attached to the ground fabric with wide-apart buttonhole stitches. The parts of the design which were too small to be cut and applied are embroidered directly from the appliqué to the ground, using perhaps chain or stem stitch. This continuation of stitchery from the appliqué element to the background fabric adds to the unity of the design.

Fig. 3. Varied stitches can be used in applying the patches.

18. An early seventeenth century French panel pictures a flower arrangement in a vase. The onlay is yellow-brown velvet; the ground is blue cloth. *Victoria and Albert Museum.*

19. *(Opposite)* The daffodil, a recognizable floral design probably copied from a herbal, dates back to the 1600's. Silver-gilt thread and silk embroidery on linen are applied to dark brown velvet with cross, long-armed cross, and couching. Flowers are yellow and cream; leaves, shades of pale green and yellow; outlines, silver-gilt and dark brown. *Victoria and Albert Museum.*

20. Old herbals inspired floral motifs in which the roots of the plant as well as the leaves and flowers were embroidered. One such example, the cornflower, is silver thread and silk embroidery on linen laid on cream silk with cross stitch and couching outlined with silver. Flowers are in two shades of blue and white; leaves, shades of green and yellow; roots, dark brown and buff. *Victoria and Albert Museum.*

Detached Appliqué

To increase their three-dimensional quality, flowers, birds, animals, and representational and abstract motifs of all kinds may be attached only in part to the ground fabric. You will have to cut a double appliqué to make a front and back for each element, adding ¼″ for seams. Stitch the front and back all around by their edges, trim and turn, then attach securely to the background with a few stitches in the center of the flower, along the inside line of the fish or butterfly skeleton, etc. A decorative embroidery stitch may be used at the place of attachment if desired.

Iron-on and Patching Appliqué

Iron-on patches, available in a wide range of color and texture, make quick appliqués. Trace the design onto the patch, grouping the elements as closely as possible to save material. Following the directions on the package, apply the cut-out patches to the ground which you are patching. Iron on as directed. Iron-on patches are not as resistant to washing as one would like them to be but they are quickly and easily replaced.

One can also cut pieces of sturdy denims, ginghams or cottons into pretty shapes such as animals, stars, nursery figures, etc. to use as patches for mending torn children's clothes. The patch is simply placed *over* the torn or frayed area, a backing such as cotton is placed *underneath* and the design is then outlined by machine with a zigzag or satin stitch. If patching by hand, use a close satin or buttonhole stitch with a strong mercerized or synthetic thread (depending upon the fabrics). Appliqué patches can also be held in place with blanket stitch. Cut the patch with no turn-down allowance.

Women's worn sweaters are another example of current appliqué usage. Tiny holes or pulls can be beautifully covered with flower or leaf designs, then embroidered with six-strand thread or silk.

Applique on Apparel

Appliqué, of course, has been used for centuries to decorate men's and women's apparel (Plates 21, 22). The bodice of a dress or an evening

21. A woman's jacket from Hungary, nineteenth century, features leather applied work. *Victoria and Albert Museum.*

22. This fragment shows bead and bullion appliqué on white silk, probably from an eighteenth century waistcoat. Lillian Freehof brought it from Paris for Bucky King, her collaborator on *Embroideries and Fabrics for Synagogue and Home*, also published by Hearthside.

23. *(Opposite)* An example of inlay, late sixteenth century Italian counterchange, shows the same design cut through two contrasting materials. They are then pieced together and the junctions sewn with cord. One pilaster hanging is red on yellow;the counterchange is yellow on red. *Victoria and Albert Museum.*

blouse can be appliquéd, embroidered with non-tarnishing silver or gold thread, and finally trimmed with beads, pearls or sequins.

Inlay

Inlay or inlaid work is appliqué in reverse. Instead of cutting out and stitching an appliqué fabric to a ground fabric, you cut away the ground fabric, following a definite pattern, to reveal another fabric beneath it. In a variation of inlay, both background and pattern are cut out and then laid on an entire foundation.

In inlaid work both design and background are cut from different materials, and the intersected parts, which resemble a jigsaw puzzle, are stitched to a foundation material underneath them both.

24. Another example of counterchange, this one was built up from a single unit. It is red velvet and cloth of gold applied work, probably French sixteenth century. *Victoria and Albert Museum.*

25. *(Opposite)* A handsome example of layered inlay, the work of San Blas Indians in Brazil, nineteenth century. Five layers of cotton material are pierced with a cutout design to show the different colors — red, orange, blue, black, pink — producing an almost quilted effect. *Collection of Bucky King.*

There are several techniques for doing inlaid work, but all of them demand accuracy in cutting out the pattern and ground, otherwise the two parts will not fit properly when laid in place, and it will be impossible to cover the joinings with edging or stitchery.

Counterchanging

This method (also known as alternating) saves costly materials and labor. In counterchanging, the material from which the cut-out was made is used, rather than discarded. The appliqué portion of one design becomes the ground pattern of the other. This kind of work was practiced by Italian workers in the Middle Ages who alternated superb velvets and satins to produce magnificent wall hangings of unusual intricacy.

Layered Inlay

This style of appliqué practiced by the San Blas Indian women produces not only a very durable fabric, but also an almost quilted effect. Several layers of the same size fabric are put together and the design sections cut out of the fabric in succeeding layers, exposing the various colors under each layer.

Method for Inlay

1. Lay four large pieces of cotton of equal size together and pin at the edges.

2. Cut a shape through the first layer exposing the layer directly under it. Snip the edges so that they can be folded under and blind hem.

3. Now, cut through both the first and second layers to expose the third layer, and cut the edges to turn under and blind hem.

4. Finally cut through all three top layers to expose the bottom fabric and color, trim the edges and blind hem in place.

5. If this is done over the entire piece, many intricate patterns and designs can be produced. Padded and quilted effects may be intro-

26. *(Opposite)* Layered inlay combined with surface stitchery in a contemporary version of appliqué by San Blas Indians. Changes in texture are obtained when successive layers of fabric are cut out. Surface stitchery (feather, fly, stem, buttonhole) enhances the various units. Heavy string quilting inserted from the wrong side pads the areas around the eyes. *Mrs. R. H. Schreiber.*

27. Inlay appliqué, buttonhole stitch outlines, with heavy handmade cords couched to fabric surface for hair — all add up to "Cleo." *Bucky King.*

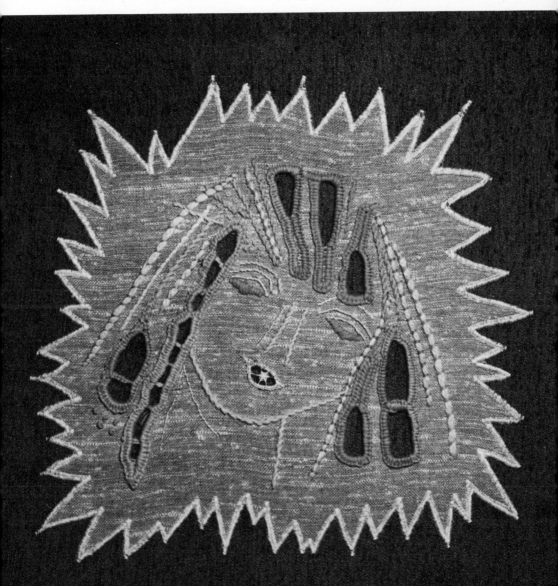

duced by padding certain areas of the design from the back of the work and inserting cording into shapes in the manner of Italian quilting.

Appliqué on Net

Appliqué on net can be used for borders and insertions on curtains, bedspreads, cushions, etc. It is also suitable as a dress trimming, for which a finer net is used. For this kind of appliqué, outline the design in chain stitches on white or colored opaque material. Carefully cut away the outside of the chain stitch, after the work is finished, leaving the design in relief on the net. When bold, extremely clear designs are chosen, the effect is particularly good.

First trace the design on muslin or stiff paper. Tack the net firmly over the design and tack the cotton in position on top. The outlines of the design should show clearly through both cotton and net. With a medium-sized mercerized cotton then outline the entire design and important markings in chain stitches.

When the work is completed, cut away the cotton around the outside of the design with sharp, pointed scissors.

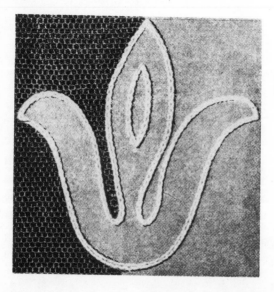

28. Appliqué on net

Appliqué for Lingerie

Ready motifs are often available at needlework shops. They may be applied on any of the lightweight fabrics used for underwear. Matching threads are generally most satisfactory but perhaps you will prefer a contrasting color to heighten the effect. It may sometimes be better to put the net over the material, so the design shows through for working, as net is more easily cut away invisibly on the right side than other material.

Work the outlines of the design in either overcast or buttonhole stitch and cut away the unwanted material on one side and the net that is not required on the other.

Machine Appliqué

Today's modern sewing machines offer limitless possibilities for both onlay and inlay. Any shape or arrangement, no matter how intricate, can be applied by machine. Two basic approaches may be used. The presser foot may be left on the machine and the fabric shapes cut and pinned to the base fabric. Basting is not necessary as the presser foot will ride easily over the pins. Both open and closed satin stitch (zigzag) may be used together with plain straight stitch. Chain stitch on the newer models is also very effective. The presser foot may also be removed and the machine may be operated for free machine stitching, using both open and closed satin stitch, straight stitch and chain. The advantage of this method is obvious, since the presser foot's removal allows the fabric to move in all directions. When the presser foot is removed, *always lower or engage the presser foot lever or bar to* insure proper tension. Check your sewing machine instruction booklet for proper setting for individual machines.

For Onlay Appliqué

It is only necessary to cut shapes $1/4$-inch larger than the actual design. All onlay shapes may be pinned to the base fabric and then stitched directly on the machine. Closed satin stitch is most often used

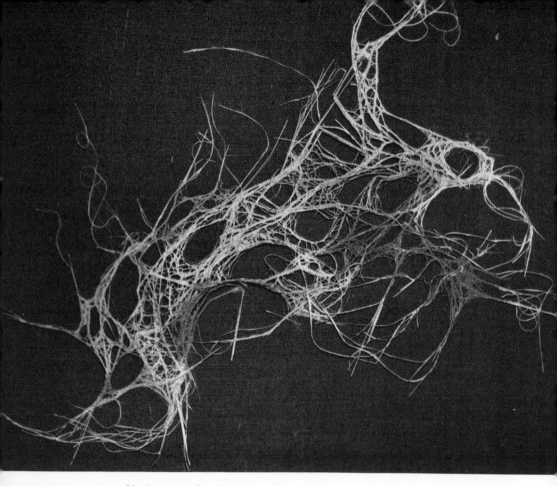

29. An example of free machine appliqué. Several forms have been machine stitched with #50 sewing thread over pliable wire, appliquéd together, then shaped. Finally, the whole piece was appliquéd to a base fabric. *Everett K. Sturgeon.*

and covers the raw edge of the applied piece with a permanent seal. Those machines having disks and cam patterns may be set to these specific patterns to produce interesting edge textures. Using the machine without the presser foot allows for a much wider range of textural treatment as it becomes very easy to "draw" scallops, loops, and pointed edges on the various applied shapes with the moving needle.

For Inlay Appliqué

Two methods are possible. The fabric may have the design sections cut out to actual size and using satin stitch, set at the widest angle, stitched directly to the ground fabric. A few pins will hold the pieces together firmly while the stitching takes place and the raw edge is neatly covered. A second method involves cutting the shape out $\frac{1}{2}$ inch larger than the finished shape and turning under the edge. The edge is then pinned to the base fabric and various patterns of straight stitching (running the machine without the presser foot) may be used to anchor the shape to the base fabric. This method is very suitable for the older style machines which do not have satin stitch attachments.

Net Inlay

This is very easily handled on the machine in both satin and straight stitch. The desired shape is first cut out of the base fabric, and the net is pinned to it from the reverse side. The two pieces are then put under the machine and satin stitch is worked over the raw edge, securing both the net and raw edge in one operation. If straight stitch is used, several rows must be made around the entire shape. When all work is completed, the fabric is turned over and the excess net carefully cut away from the reverse side.

Cords, Ribbons and Braids

These may also be applied by machine, using either straight stitch or fancy satin stitch patterns. Wools and applied threads offer many texture possibilities when loosely applied with open satin or zigzag stitch. Cords may be anchored tightly at one end with heavy satin stitch and left frayed out and unstitched at the other end. Loops may be formed in the same fashion from ribbon or heavy wool by stitching only in specified places.

Stitching Effects

Besides the already mentioned straight and satin stitch, other stitching methods are also possible, such as cording and whipping. Check the

book of instructions for setting your machine tension properly to produce these effects.

Ecclesiastical Appliqué

Appliqué has been used in ecclesiastical embroidery from the early
Middle Ages to the present day. Middle European villages, lacking the
beneficence of a local noble patron, used appliqué in imitation of
costly woven tapestries, and as a pictorial device for relating Bible
stories to those unable to read. Gold work, traditionally associated with
ecclesiastical embroidery and used in church vestments as early as the
tenth century, is nothing but a special process of onlay appliqué. In our
modern world, ecclesiastical appliqué serves a truly functional purpose, adding both color and texture to articles too large or impractical
for surface stitchery only. Machine appliqué is especially suitable for
large Dossal hangings, Ark curtains, and banners that would otherwise
require many long hours of tedious surface stitchery. Both onlay and
inlay methods may be used successfully, in combination or separately.
It is not possible here to develop the full method of metal thread tech-
nique, since it is a highly specialized process, but a brief list of sug-
gested materials is offered:

Onlay Appliqué Materials

Gold and silver cords and braids
lamé, gold and silver kid
silks, velvets, and textured weaves of all kinds
linens and cottons, wools, synthetics

Items Suitable for Appliqué

Christian—Altar frontals, chasubles, dossal hangings, banners, ante-
             pendium hangings, copes, miters, funeral palls, stoles
Hebrew—Ark curtains, Tora mantels, pulpit desk covers, tallis, hang-
             ings, tefillen bags, ark valance.
A story can be quickly told in appliqué, using simple shapes, and thus

30. *(Left)* "Alleluia," an ecclesiastical hanging, is fashioned from light brown rayon appliqué on an ochre linen background. The stitchery is done in wool and silk of varied colors and the entire work is mounted on burlap with fringe. *Sister M. Helena, O. S. F.*

31. *(Right)* The Palm Sunday procession is shown here on a background of maroon homespun. The appliqué is figured cotton in gold and oranges, and the stitchery is in wools and silks of green, reds, and gray. *Sister M. Helena, O. S. F.*

32. "His Name Shall Be Called Emmanuel"—surface stitchery and appliqué in leather and other fabrics. *Sister M. Helena, O. S. F.*

an image is presented to the viewer, directing the mind to worship. The cross shown in Plate 34 is applied in leatherette to a raw silk chasuble in satin stitch, an effective reminder of Calvary. The banner, "His Name Shall Be Called Emmanuel," designed and worked by Sister Helena, O.S.F., Alverno College, Milwaukee, Wisconsin, quickly tells the story of Christmas and the Nativity.

33. Here rayon provides the background for appliqué in cotton and homespun. Colors used are tan, gold, orange, reds, yellow-green and blue-green in the appliqué and yarn stitchery; leather fringes the neutral ground. *Sister M. Helena, O. S. F.*

34. This raw silk priest's chasuble has a leatherette cross appliquéd to the front and back with embroidery stitch. *R. A. Newhouse, Inc.*

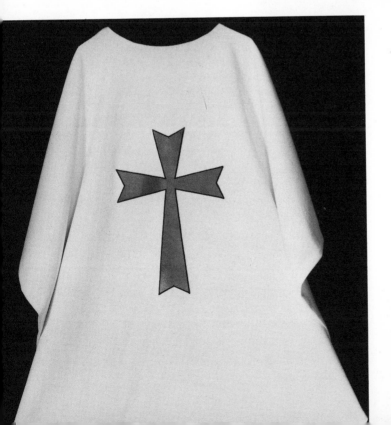

ℬ Bead, Braid, Ribbon and Cord Appliqué

Cord and braids have many uses in laid-on appliqué. They are suitable as edgings, to outline various decorative elements, to raise the surface of the embroidery and for other uses. Jewels and beads of different kinds are appropriate not only in ecclesiastical and traditional appliqué, but also to add the textural quality which is one of the signposts of modern work.

Bead Appliqué

Beadwork is one of the earliest forms of onlay appliqué, probably practiced by cave men to fasten interesting stones, seeds, bits of bones, and sea shells to their garments. Many primitive civilizations used beads as a trading device. Polished and strung on belts and sashes, beads were the wampum of North American Indians, who placed twice the value on black beads as on white.

Church vestments have long been decorated with beads and jewels. One famous example is the "mantel of the Golden Fleece" in which real pearls are used. In *Embroideries and Fabrics for Synagogue and Home,* by Lillian S. Freehof and Bucky King, an ark curtain, said to be the oldest in the world, shows beadwork.

35. In this hanging, marbles are attached to the base fabric with detached buttonhole stitching. Threads are drawn and pulled and many of the with-drawn threads are regrouped and attached with couching methods to the surface. Heavy cords are also appliquéd to ground. *Marie T. Kelly.*

Beads or bugles, as they were once called, come in every size, shape and material. They can be made of bits of glass, wood, metal, plastic, bone, shell, cork, rubber, leather, iridescent sequins and spangles, and even papier mâché. They are made in every size and shape with round, square and rectangular being the most common.

Bead Methods

Beads are threaded either on a cord or fine string and applied to the ground fabric by stitching down the cord, or they are stitched down individually or in groups, using the stitching needle and thread as the application method (see drawing). They may also be knotted, woven,

Fig. 4. Bead designs over fine wire: (a) 3-looped form shaped and ready to apply; (b) circular motif, showing wire join at center bead; (c) pattern of square beads and wire, ready for appliqué; (d) appliqué with several beads before a stitch is taken, method of Southwest Indians; (e) stitching down each bead to fabric; (f) threading through bead and then stitching; (g) a vermicelli pattern.

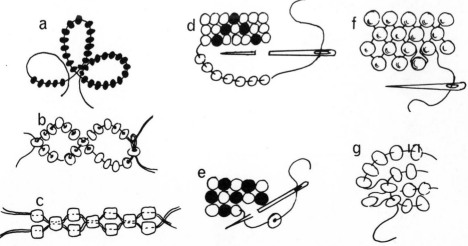

36. A jewel panel in onlay appliqué uses velvets, silks, metallic braids, fake jewels, and different kinds of beads including jets and bugles. *Mrs. Hans Rudolph.*

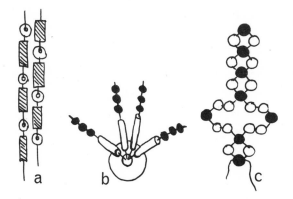

Fig. 5. Examples of allover bead motifs: (a) bugle beads and round beads; (b) sequins, bugle beads, and round beads; (c) shaped bead pattern for appliqué.

Fig. 6. Two methods for stringing beads and stitching them to the surface: (a) stitching the holding string after each bead; (b) stitching the holding string after 2 or 3 beads.

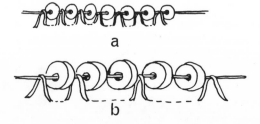

and strung over fine wire to make freestanding effects. They may be ued to create geometric all-over patterns, to add highlights, or to produce shaded effects, as in the Berlin wool bead embroidery. They are sometimes combined with sequins, flat metal shapes, seeds, stones, pearls, and all manner of natural as well as man-made materials.

Braidwork

Braids—plaited threads, ribbons and cords—have been used in all ages and in most countries. They make a neat and decorative edging; they strengthen the article to which they are applied; and they are a good substitute for embroidery, being inexpensive and easily stitched down. If the braids are interwoven with gold and silver threads, the edging adds brilliance and luster to the design.

Sew on the braids with invisible stitches, taking care when rounding a corner to work on the inside edge so it lies flat. To conceal the stitches, insert the needle between strands that have been separated slightly.

Ribbon and Cord Appliqué

A wide variety of ribbons, cords and rick-racks are now available in both natural and synthetic materials. Many different methods of application may be utilized.

Fig. 7. Ribbon appliqué: (a) strips of ribbon secured with herringbone stitch; (b) fabric or ribbon secured with buttonhole insertion; (c) and (d) rick rack couched with fly stitch; (e) rick rack couched with back stitch and detached chain.

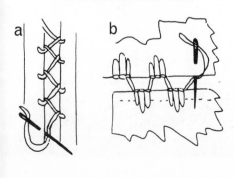
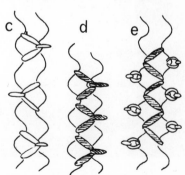

37. *(Top)* Onlay cord appliqué using a variety of fabrics and handmade cords of both wool and hemp. *Mrs. Ruth Cover.*

38. *(Bottom)* A hanging shows onlay appliqué with wool thread on cotton fabrics. *Mrs. Ruth Cover.*

For Direct Ribbon Appliqué

Lay the ribbon directly on the base fabric, folding and shaping it to create different forms and anchoring it to the base with tiny stitches.

Ribbon can also be laced in rows to the base fabric with such stitches as herringbone or cretan stitch. Fabric may be created by using an insertion stitch, such as buttonhole, and several rows of ribbon, all held together with the buttonhole insertion.

Fig. 8. Ribbon and rick rack appliqué: (a) several rows of corded ribbon laced together; (b) plain ribbon laid down and blind stitched in fan shape; (c) buttonhole used to couch ribbon; (d) plain rick rack; (e) plain rick rack used in double row couched with fly stitch.

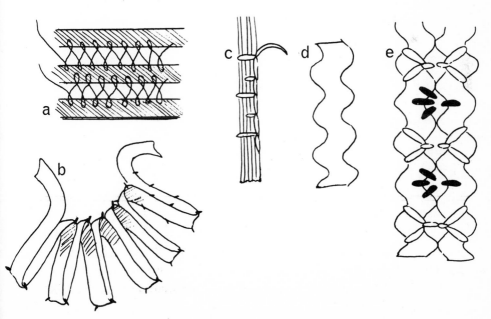

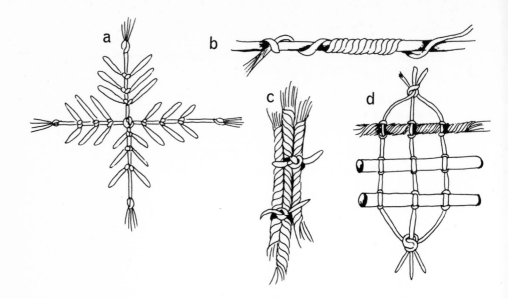

Fig. 9. Onlay cords made from twine and strings: (a) a cross shape made by knotting on 3 side pieces to each cross bar; (b) making a wrapped cord of thin string over a heavy cord; (c) heavy cords tied together with knots; (d) string used to knot heavy cord and plastic straws.

Fancy Cord Appliqué

All manner of cord, rick-rack, and ribbon may be appliquéd to base fabrics. Note the selection of embroidery stitches on the sketches showing rick-rack couched with chain, fly and back stitch.

Making Your Own Appliqué Cords

Experiment with ordinary strings and cords from hardware stores and markets. Once the desired effect is obtained, more expensive cords may be substituted. The 4- and 6-ply cords can be frayed out easily to create many fan shapes and even donkey tails. All manner of strings and cords may be twisted together to make thicker cords. Knotted strings make very interesting effects and are easily created by tying simple knots in various thicknesses and combinations of strings. Both a simple single knot and a fancy rolled knot are shown. Back looping is also quite effective (see Fig. 10).

Many forms of appliqué can be made by tying the string and cord together to form new shapes. A cross can be made by knotting thin strings on heavy string. Heavy cords and ropes may be tied together in interlocking sections and then used as applied shapes. Thick cord may be wrapped with finer string to produce rolled effects. Plastic straws may be tied together in string patterns and stitched down to the base fabric. Macramé knotting processes are all useful for creating your own appliqué.

Fig. 10. Cords, twine, and strings used to make forms for appliqué: (a) a heavy cord frayed out, such as for a donkey's tail; (b) 3 cords twisted together to make heavier twisted forms; (c and d) knotted twine and a simple knot; (e) back knotting twine or heavy wool; (f) a heavy twisted knot 6 wraps.

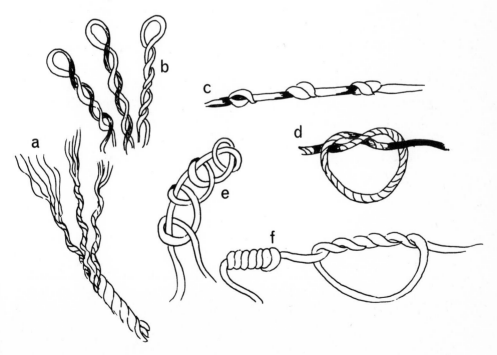

Appli-tique Bouquet in Large White Frame

You'll need for background

Picture frame 12″ x 16½″ inside opening
Corrugated board 13″ x 17½″
Linen fabric, eggshell 16″ x 20″
Glue, Sobo or Elmer's
Picture hanger
Scrap of fabric 4″ x 4″

You'll need for flowers (rick rack)

2 yds. Jumbo rick rack, white
1 yd. Jumbo rick rack, lavender
1 yd. Jumbo rick rack, pink
1½ yds. Jumbo rick rack, rose
½ yd. Jumbo rick rack, aqua
1 yd. Jumbo rick rack, copen
1¼ yds. Jumbo rick rack, emerald
⅔ yd. Jumbo rick rack, Nile
5 yds. Regular rick rack, apricot
⅔ yd. Regular rick rack, gold
1⅓ yds. Regular rick rack, orange
2 yds. Regular rick rack, yellow
⅔ yd. Regular rick rack, purple
2⅔ yds. Regular rick rack, canary
⅔ yd. Regular rick rack, lavender
1⅓ yds. Regular rick rack, lt. blue
½ yd. Baby rick rack, Nile
¼ yd. Baby rick rack, rose
⅔ yd. Baby rick rack, white
½ yd. Baby rick rack, copen
½ yd. Baby rick rack, lavender
⅔ yd. Baby rick rack, lt. blue
½ yd. Baby rick rack, pink
1 yd. Baby rick rack, yellow
2 yds. Tubing, avocado

Background:

1. Thin glue to consistency of milk. Use nail brush and lightly paint entire surface of cardboard with glue solution. Allow to partially dry. Center fabric over surface and smooth out evenly.

39. Appli-tique wall hanging. *Wm. E. Wright Co.*

2. Turn over to wrong side. Fold long sides snugly over cardboard and glue to back. Fold and glue short sides, cutting away excess fabric under fold at corners.

For flower placement:

1. Mark 1″ squares on tracing paper in size of frame opening.

2. Place location marks on squares as shown and transfer to background (use dressmaker tracing paper).

3. Make all flowers first, also stems where needed and leaves.

4. Glue stems in place, then flowers and leaves following tracing. Add forget-me-nots at random.

Mount unit into frame by holding with fine nails on reverse side. Seal entire back with one sheet of firm paper glued to frame back. Add picture hanger to back.

Key for quantity of flowers needed and Key for flower letter (see diagram opposite)

Key for color numbers

Quantity	Letter	
5	a. Double Petal Daisy	1 White
1	b. Pom-pom	2 Copen Blue
1	c. Giant Zinnia	3 Avocado
6	d. Baby Mum	4 Emerald
8	e. Buttercup	5 Gold
6	f. Violet	6 Lavender
2	g. Flower Spike	7 Lt. Blue
6	h. Leaf Cluster	8 Nile Green
24	i. Leaf	9 Orange
See diagram	j. Stem	10 Pink
See diagram	k. Slim Stem	11 Apricot
See diagram	l. Baby Rick Rack Stem	12 Purple
24	o. Forget-me-nots:	13 Rose
	6 ea. white and Light Blue	14 Aqua
	4 ea. Copen, Lavender, Pink	15 Yellow
		16 Canary

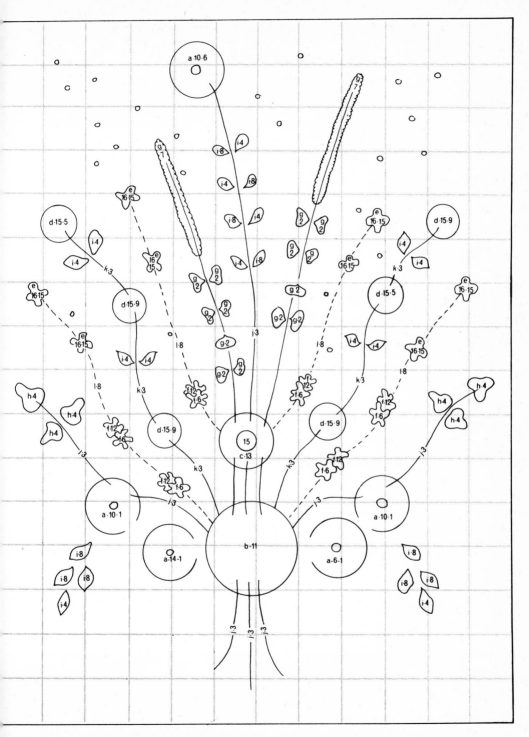

Fig. 11. Diagram for Appli·tique Bouquet, Plate 39. Scale: ½″ = 1″.

Double Petal Daisy

You'll need for outer petals: ½ yd. Jumbo Rick Rack, White
½ yd. Jumbo Rick Rack, Pink

You'll need for center: 6 in. Baby Rick Rack, Canary

To make outer petals:

1. Place white over pink with points matching and pink showing slightly at lower edge. Cut ends should be in downward direction. Cut away if necessary. Stitch in and out center of each point. Ease rick rack if needed to make points coincide.

2. Draw thread snugly and seam raw ends on wrong side of flower.

3. Stitch through each folded point around inner circle and draw thread snugly to hold shape.

To make center
(see illustrations page 74):

1. There must be an even number of points along upper edge with cut ends in downward direction. Cut away if necessary.

2. Stitch in one point and out the next point along upper edge, building all points on needle.

3. Pull thread through leaving 3 in. free at knotted end.

4. Tie thread together from both ends to form tight circle.

5. Tack center in place

Pom-Pom

You'll need: 4 in. square scrap of fabric
5 yds. Rick Rack, Yellow

To make:

1. Fold strip in half to 2½ yds.* Starting at folded end, interlock rick
rack by hooking "V's" together.

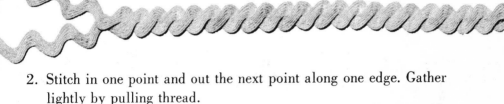

2. Stitch in one point and out the next point along one edge. Gather
lightly by pulling thread.

3. Draw a 3 in. diameter circle on scrap fabric.

4. Tack inner gathered points to circle and continue to center in spiral
leaving outer edges of rick rack raised and free.

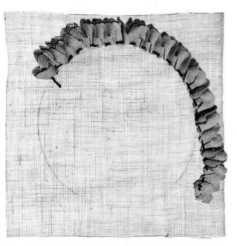

5. Clip away excess fabric.

*If rick rack is on 3 yd. cards, cut two lengths, 2½ yds. long, then interlock together.

Giant Zinnia

You'll need for outer petals: 1 yd. Jumbo Rick Rack, Rose

You'll need for center: 4½ in. Baby Rick Rack, Rose
$\qquad$ ⅓ yd. Baby Rick Rack, Yellow

To make outer petals:

1. Use rose jumbo rick rack. There must be an even number of points along upper edge with cut ends in downward direction. Cut away if necessary.

2. Stitch in one point and out the next point along upper edge, building points on needle.

3. Pull thread through leaving 3 in. free at knotted end. Repeat steps #2 and #3 to end of rick rack.

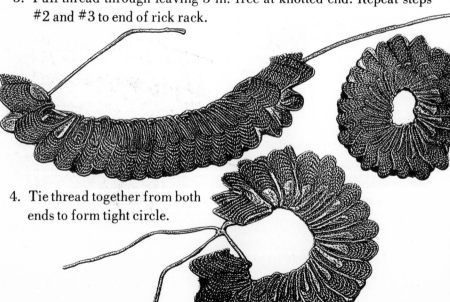

4. Tie thread together from both ends to form tight circle.

To make center:

1. Use rose baby rick rack and follow #1, 2, 3, and 4 above.

2. Use yellow baby rick rack and follow #1, 2, and 3 above.

3. Wrap yellow rick rack around rose and tie thread together to form tight circle.

4. Tack center in place.

Straight Stem-Tubing

You'll need: Tubing
          Desired length plus ¼ in. for each stem

To make:

1. Draw stem line on fabric.

2. Work ¼ in. of filler cord out of one raw end. Clip away cord.

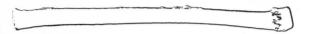

3. Tack back empty casing at other end. Use for exposed end of stem.

4. Baste tubing over stem line.

5. Tack tubing from wrong side of fabric.

6. Remove basting.

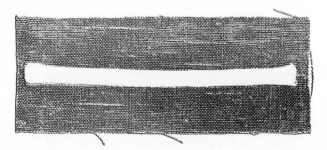

Baby Mum

You'll need: ⅓ yd. Regular Rick Rack, gold
⅓ yd. Regular Rick Rack, yellow

To make:

1. Fold rick rack to half length and interlock by hooking "V's" together.

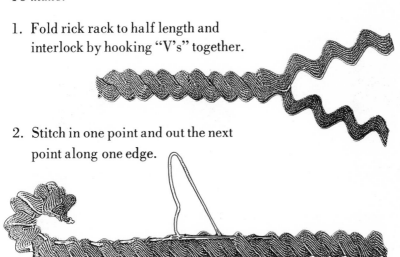

2. Stitch in one point and out the next point along one edge.

3. Draw thread snugly. Coil and tack through center.

Buttercup

You'll need for outer petals: ⅓ yd. Rick Rack, Canary Yellow

To make outer petals:

1. Cut 4 points of rick rack with cut ends in upward direction.

2. Seam to form ring.   3. Cut away seam allowance.

4. With same thread tack lower points together.

5. Repeat 1 through 4 above and tack one cup inside the other.

You'll need for center: 2 in. Baby Rick Rack, Yellow

To make center:

1. There must be an odd number of points along upper edge with one
    end in upward direction and other end in downward direction.

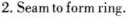

2. Stitch into upper "V" and out lower "V" building rick rack on
    needle.

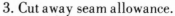

3. Pull thread through keeping rick rack vertical and leaving 3 in.
    free at knotted end.

4. Tie thread together from both ends to form tight circle keeping rick rack ends to underside.

5. Cut away excess rick rack ends and shape with fingers making sure all petals are vertical.

6. Tack center in place.

Violet

You'll need: 4 in. Rick Rack, Lavender

To make:

1. Cut 6 points of rick rack having cut ends in downward direction.

2. Seam to form ring. Cut away excess seam allowance.

3. With same thread stitch in and out each upper point of ring.

4. Draw snugly and tack at center.

5. Turn to right side. Cup 3 upper points upward and 2 lower points downward.

Flower Spike

You'll need for Stem: ⅓ to ½ yd. Tubing

To make Stem:

1. Draw stem line on fabric.

2. Baste tubing over stem line.

3. Tack tubing from wrong side of fabric.

4. Remove basting.

You'll need for upper flowers: ⅔ yd. Regular Rick Rack, Lt. Blue

To make upper flowers:

1. Run stitches through center of regular size rick rack. Draw thread snugly. Gathered strip should measure about 6½ inches.

2. Pin evenly on each side of stem keeping gathered strip flat. Tack in place.

You'll need for lower flowers: ½ yd. Jumbo Rick Rack, Copen

To make lower flowers:

1. Cut a "W" of Jumbo rick rack.

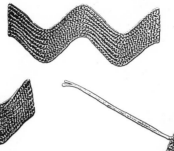

2. Seam to form ring.

3. With same thread run stitches around upper edge of ring.

4. Draw snugly and tack at center.

5. Make 7 blossoms and tack to both sides of stem with seamed ends toward fabric.

Leaf Cluster

You'll need for leaves: Jumbo Rick Rack

To make leaves:

1. Cut 2 points of rick rack with cut ends in upward direction.

2. Seam to form ring.

3. With same thread stitch through upper points of ring.

4. Draw snugly and tack at center.

5. Stitch inner "V's" together.

6. Turn completed leaf to right side.

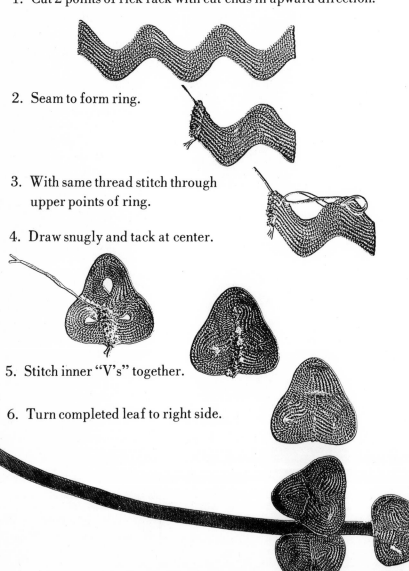

Rick Rack Leaf

You'll need: "W" of Jumbo Rick Rack

To make:

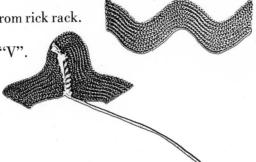

1. Cut a "W" from rick rack.

2. Seam lower "V".

3. Fold in raw ends and tack. Cut away extending raw points.

4. Turn to right side.

To make a slim stem (k):

1. Remove filler cord from tubing length needed.

2. Fold tubing in half (or roll between fingers) and hand tack for stem half as thick as regular stem.

Forget-me-not

You'll need: 4″ Baby Rick Rack, Copen

To make:

1. There must be an even number of points along upper edge with cut ends in downward direction. Cut away if necessary.

2. Stitch in one point and out the next point along upper edge, building all points on needle.

3. Pull thread through leaving 3 in. free at knotted end.

4. Tie thread together from both ends to form tight circle.

Stems—Baby Rick Rack

You'll need: Desired-length Baby Rick Rack, Emerald

To make:

1. Draw design on fabric.

2. Stitch through center of rick rack to design or glue rick rack to design.

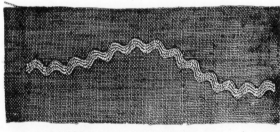

4 Appliqué and Patchwork Quilts

Appliqué is often confused with patchwork but they are separate forms of needlework, both using pieces of material. In appliqué, the pieces are applied to another fabric. In patchwork, the pieces are sewn together, edges to edges, so that they form one overall mosaic. Many quilts combine both forms of needlework.

The earliest type of patchwork quilt was "crazy quilt," a collection of odd scraps of fabric used because they were there. This was followed by quilts in which fabric scraps were selected with some consideration for design, then cut into geometric shapes and pieced together. Quilts like this require no great skill, but they do require time and care. One such quilt is shown in Plate 43. It utilizes three shapes: squares and large and small triangles. The lines can be kept straight and the quilt flat without too much difficulty, provided you cut so that all the shapes are uniform in size and true to the grain of the fabric. If, for example, some triangles are cut from the lengthwise grain and some from the bias of the fabric, the bias pieces would stretch when you did the piecing. Directions for making a quilt follow.

Pieced Tops

Making a Pattern

Trace the design onto a sheet of tracing or bond paper. Cut out along tracing line. Place the paper on glazed blotter or sand paper and, holding it firmly in left hand, cut around it as shown in Fig. 12A. Make two or more blotter or sandpaper patterns at one time so that when one is worn you will have at least one replacement. (Sandpaper and blotter are equally good; they both hold the fabric so it doesn't shift while you cut it.)

Fig. 12. (a) Cut design from heavy paper; (b) trace required number of units on fabric; (c) cut out units; (d) press back seam allowance.

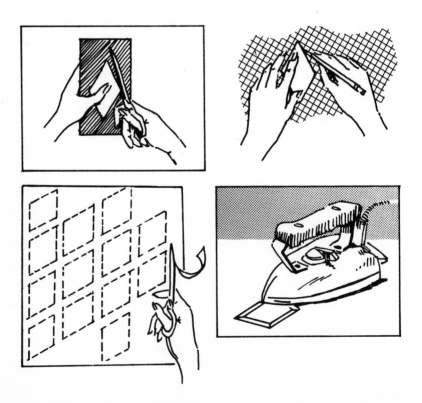

Cutting the fabric

Even off the fabric by pulling a thread across it. Press thoroughly, using a damp cloth if necessary to remove wrinkles. Place the pattern on the lengthwise grain of the material. A square should be placed on the true lengthwise and crosswise grain; a diamond so that the two opposite sides are on the lengthwise grain, otherwise there would be four bias sides and these are hard to piece without stretching (Fig. 12B). Trace required number of units one-half inch apart on all sides. Cut out each unit with ¼-inch seam allowance on all sides (Fig. 12C). Place pattern on the wrong side of the cut fabric. Using a moderately hot iron, press back the seam allowance to make a sharp guide line for sewing (Fig. 12D). Keep pieces of same kind together. Running a thread through the pile is the old-fashioned way to do it; it still works!

Sewing units together

Always join units from the center out. Join by stitching units together to form blocks. Use a running stitch on wrong side (Fig. 13). A thread

Fig. 13. Sewing units together.

about 18 inches long is the correct length. Press seams frequently as you work to improve appearance of quilt. Join blocks in strips, then sew strips together until you have completed the top. Sew the border on last.

Appliqué Quilts

If the quilt design is complicated, trace or stamp it onto the quilt top to show where the appliqués are to be placed.

To make stems

Use bias strips 1½ inches wide, folded twice, as shown in Fig. 14A.

In cutting appliqué parts, remember to clip in well to the fold on the curves in order to make the pieces lie flat. To make stems, use bias strips 1½ inches wide folded twice as shown in Fig. 14B.

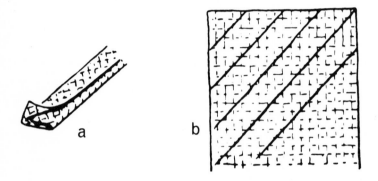

Fig. 14. Making stems: (a) bias strips folded twice; (b) cut bias strips as shown.

Applying Designs

The most important consideration in making an appliqué quilt is to apply the design in its correct position. To do this the block may be creased in such a way as to provide guide lines for laying on the design.

Fig. 15A. Fold in half and crease with thumb nail.

Fig. 15B. Unfold and fold in the opposite direction and crease.

Fig. 15C. Fold from corner to corner.

Fig. 15D. Fold from corner to corner in the opposite direction.

Fig. 15E. Shows the creases made by the various folds.

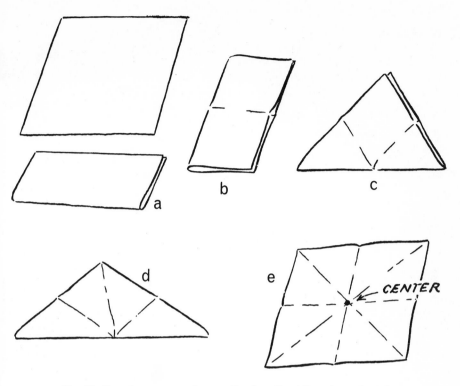

Fig. 15. Creasing squares for appliqué quilts (directions above).

All designs are applied in relation to the center and to the lines which have been creased. Specific directions are given with quilt, p. 94. Leaf ends are tucked under stems, stem ends are covered with buds or flowers, and all raw ends are turned under.

When applying curved unit, baste ⅛-inch away from outside edge and pull slightly to form curved edge; or clip well into the fold on the curves to make the pieces lie flat.

When entire design has been basted in place, sew around the edge with a small, invisible stitch using mercerized sewing threads of matching colors. Take care not to pull stitches too tightly because this puckers the material.

40. Stamped quilt showing the appliqué design and quilting pattern, and including patches stamped with cutting and turning. *Bucilla.*

Quilt Making by Sewing Machine

In using a modern sewing machine with a variety of stitches you may cut actual-size pieces on the marked lines and join them with a close zigzag stitch. Or, cut your pieces slightly larger, join with a zigzag stitch following the marked lines, and cut away the extra material from the outside with finely pointed sharp scissors. If your machine does not have a variety of stitches, you must allow for at least ¼-inch seams when cutting. In piecing, join the parts following the marked lines on the back. In appliquéing, turn under the ¼-inch seams, place in the proper location and baste, later stitching to the background close to the edges.

Cut the background squared for the top with ¼-inch seams all around. It is important to mark accurately and avoid stretching of the materials. This is particularly true when your pattern involves diamonds or perfectly round pieces.

As you acquire skill in this work you will find that it is not necessary to baste; you may simply pin the pieces into position, since most modern machines sew right over straight pins. This will eliminate much of the work of making a quilt.

For additional beauty in doing appliqué work, padding of the appliqué parts will accentuate the design. To do this, leave a small section unstitched and pad with extra cotton, pushing it under the appliquéd parts with a knitting needle until firm. Finish the stitching to complete the appliqué.

Assembling the Quilt by Machine

If your quilt is designed so that it may be made by blocks, I suggest that you piece or appliqué each block and quilt it as a unit. Do not try to appliqué, quilt and join all at one time unless the pattern is extremely simple, for such a procedure would take all the "puffing" out of the quilting and flatten your quilt. When the top of the block is finished, mark the quilting design on it, leaving ⅜ inch unquilted. Cut the material for the back into squares of the same dimensions as the pieced or appliquéd top. Next cut your cotton ¼ inch smaller than the material for the backing. Baste or pin the back, cotton and top together securely

41 and 42. Designs of fanciful trees like this are always appealing. Plate 41, left: an original design made in Mexico featuring appliqué work and stitchery on heavy cotton. Below, a stamped pattern. *F. Schumacher, Bucilla.*

43. Patchwork coverlet with border of applied motifs made from cutout chintz flowers. *Victoria and Albert Museum.*

with the cotton centered between top and back. Quilt with a fine stitch (10 to 12 stitches to an inch) to within ⅜ inch of the edge. For a more elaborate quilt, use embroidery stitches to do the quilting.

These finished blocks are then joined together. The cotton will be ¼ inch from the edges of the material all around. Fold the top and the back edges over each other so that the edges of the cotton meet. Keeping the seams in a line, stitch together. These seams may be covered by an interlocking border of a matching or contrasting color. When the entire quilt has been assembled, clip the rough edges and bind with the same color as that used for the interlocking borders.

Never before have there been so many possibilities for elaborate quilting. Modern sewing machines with their great variety of stitches make beautiful designs themselves. A new combination zipper and cording foot which is adjustable allows you to sew on the left or right of your needle. These are available for many machines and prevent having to pull so much of the material under the arm of the machine.

Of course there will come a time when you will have to be working in the center of your quilt. Half of the quilt should be pulled under the foot and rolled tightly in the center of the machine while this part of the quilting is done.

The important thing in quilting on your sewing machine is to baste the backing, cotton and top securely. Start at the center and baste to the edges no more than 4 inches apart. This helps to keep the quilt smooth and avoids puckering.

Making The President's Wreath

Materials

8½ yds. of white 39″ wide, 9½ yds. of green, 3 yds. of red.

Each block is made up of 5 different units. Patterns are given for half of Unit Nos. 1, 2 and 3; Unit No. 4 is complete; Unit No. 5 is made by drawing 2 circles inside each other, the larger circle 16¼″ in diameter and the smaller circle 14⅝″ in diameter. Patterns are also given for half of Unit Nos. 6 and 7; these are used for border. See pp. 85-89 for general directions.

44. President's Wreath, a graceful and elegant quilt design which is popular as a bride's quilt. Directions for making it are given on pages 94-97.

To Apply Design

Place circle so that it is the same distance away from center on all sides. See p. 88 for Applying Design.

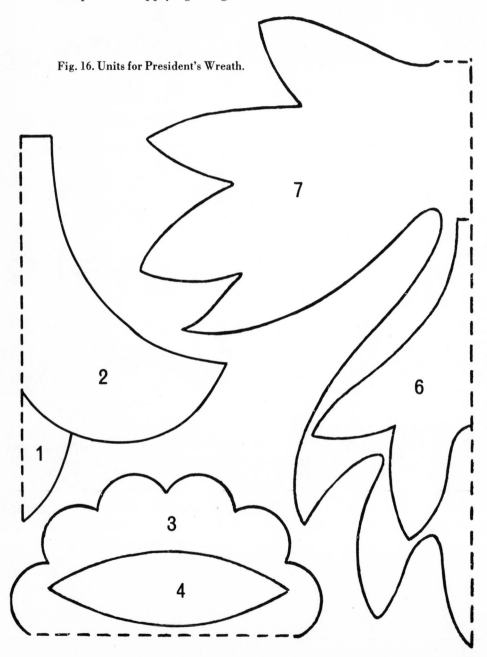

Fig. 16. Units for President's Wreath.

Fig. 17. Finished block for President's Wreath, 22½" square.

Setting the Quilt

See general directions on pp. 85-89. For border, cut 2 strips of white 12½" x 68". Sew one on each side. Then cut 2 strips 18½" x 92" and sew one across top and bottom. Using green, make six 12" scallops 12" wide and 5½" deep for each short side, and seven for each long side (use a plate or a phonograph record 12" in diameter to make the pattern). Place scallops 4" in from all edges and adjacent to each other. Make a scallop to fit each corner. Complete border by appliquéing a Unit No. 6 between each scallop and a Unit No. 7 in each scallop. Quilt as shown or as desired.

Number of Each Unit to Cut

For 1 block cut Unit No. 1 (tip of bud)—8 red; Unit No. 2 (base of bud)—8 green; Unit No. 3 (flower)—4 red; Unit No. 4 (leaf)—24 green; Unit No. 5 (circle)—1 green. Cut 9 squares of white 23" square.

5 *Teaching Appliqué to Children*

Young children love to do appliqué, and this type of embroidery can be part of a broader teaching process too. Odds and ends of fabrics, discards from Mother's sewing basket, Father's old felt hat—all of these can be cut into different shapes, then dropped onto the ground fabric at random. The units can be moved around over and over again until the desired result is achieved, at which point the appliqué may be pinned, sewed or pasted down. The relationship of shapes to each other, the ease with which a design can be changed with a movement of just a few elements, and most of all, the pleasure of using "found objects" will be part of the lesson.

Easily recognizable silhouettes and shapes of rabbits, leaves, birds, flowers, scraps of fabrics folded once or twice, then cut and unfolded (like doilies) will delight the early graders. Even in kindergarten, youngsters can learn to pick out their own smocks if an appropriate animal or their own names are appliquéd on. The holidays can be observed with various appliqué projects. For Valentine's Day, a large felt heart appliquéd on a painted cardboard with ribbon streamers, maybe with her initials stitched on too, will please the mother of even the least-apt little needleworker. For Halloween, you can make a landscape collage. Silhouette and appliqué a black cat, a witch on a broom, a cut-out orange pumpkin, and a scarecrow near a fence. Christmas motifs

45. "Justin on a Train with Beryl's Purse" was designed by four-year-old Mila Koslan Schwartz in cut construction paper and crayons and was worked by J. H. Koslan Schwartz in fabrics and threads chosen by the child. Careful tracing was required to preserve the character of the child's work.

could include tiny felt bells, rickrack bows, absorbent cotton snowmen, and real pine sprigs. For Hanukkah, a simple cut-out menorah, dreidel, or candle would symbolize the "feast of lights."

Making Banners

One of the most delightful forms of onlay appliqué for children consists of the production and creation of banners. In religious schools the subject matter can deal with a special holiday or saint day, while in the public school system, national holidays, or "game" banners, such as "tic-tac-toe", offer numerous possibilities. Boys are particularly interested in medals and small ribbon medals with four-inch medallions in appliqué present a real challenge.

Methods for children

1. Discuss a banner or medal theme.

2. Have the children prepare a "mock-up" of the fabric banner in paper, first.

3. Decide whether the appliqué will be hand or machine or whether the two methods can be combined for speed. Cut out the shapes.

4. Pin the fabric pieces to the background textile.

5. Stitch using various techniques.

Themes for banner work

1. Religious themes, saint's days, high holy days, Bible stories.

2. Banners that are games such as chess, checkers, racetrack, "pin the tail," cribbage.

3. Name banners using family names, such as "King" with crowns, gold scepters, etc.

4. Club banners, athletic banners, sports banners, etc.

Felt and Pellon Appliqué

Felt can be used to make the simplest kind of appliqué since it does not fray or ravel and therefore there is no need to turn edges under or finish them in any way. Simply pin the pieces in place (or glue them lightly) and slip stitch to the background. A background of burlap or heavy upholstery material would be in keeping. Since felt has no textural interest, added stitchery with yarn would give variety to the surface.

Pellon, like felt, also lacks texture and is made by a matting process, as opposed to a weaving one. Used as a lining in dressmaking, it comes only in white. But it can be easily dyed with colored India ink and felt-tip pens. It has many possibilities for work with children. As it is also semi-transparent, Pellon can be used to create three-dimensional effects.

Felt or Pellon Floral Pillow

Assemble your own bouquet or begin with the simple bowl holding an assortment of blossoms as in Fig. 3. It would make a bright cushion cover. Use a burlap or heavy linen as a background, and felt (or other colorful materials) for the appliqué. Cut out each flower and the bowl separately onto colored felt. Tack design units in position on the ground material. Work the outlines and flower centers in buttonhole stitch, chain stitch, satin stitch or back stitch, wih lazy daisy stitches for the stamens. The bowl should be cut and tacked on the background and invisibly hemmed so it stands out well. Then stitch the edges with wool of a contrasting shade, either in buttonhole stitch with the purl edge facing out, or in close overcasting. Press well on the wrong side after it is completed.

Machine Work in the Classroom

Children of about junior high school age who are old enough to use a sewing machine can complete the next two projects in a short time.

A Padded Potholder Set

Follow the directions for Raised or Padded Appliqué. Cut-up pieces of old nylon stockings can be used as batting.

Materials needed for a pair of potholders:

Pink denim—two 8″ circles for potholder; one piece large enough for flower; one circle, about 2¾″, for flower center.

White denim—two 8″ circles for potholder.

Pink and white gingham—one piece large enough for flower; one circle, about 2¾″, for flower center.

Dacron or cotton batting, ¾ yard.

Double Fold Bias Tape, green.

46. Padded pot holders are easily appliquéd and make charming gifts. *(Photograph by O. Philip Roedel.)*

Mercerized Sewing thread: pink, white, green.
Paper for patterns.

1. Copy the flower as shown or create your own; draw a paper pattern and cut out. Place and pin pattern to fabric. Cut as listed above.

From the batting, cut eight 8″ circles, two flowers, and two flower centers. Remove pattern and trim away ¼″ from edge of each layer of batting.

2. For each potholder, place one pink and one white 8″ circle with wrong sides together; insert four large circles of batting; pin around outer edge.

3. For one potholder, pin gingham flower with a layer of batting to white side; baste. Clip around edge of pink flower center; turn under ¼″ over small circle of batting; pin in center of flower; baste. Repeat for second potholder, with a pink flower and a gingham center.

4. Set sewing machine for a close zigzag stitch. Bobbin thread should be white; top thread, pink. Machine stitch appliqué in place, guiding edge of presser foot along edge of fabric. After stitching, carefully trim away any raw edges and remove basting.

5. Bind edge of each potholder with double fold bias tape. Cut two 2½″ strips for loops. Topstitch edges. Attach to potholder.

Laundry Bag with Jack-in-the-box Appliqué

Materials:

Cotton denim, 1 yard, 36″ wide for bag; scraps for appliqué.
Mercerized thread to match fabrics.
Cotton or Dacron batting, 1½″ yards.
Cotton cable cord for hanging bag, 1¼ yards.

Sewing:

1. Cut bag fabric to measure 32″ by 36″. Turn under 3″ along one 36″ edge (top of bag), then fold fabric to 18″ width and press folds.

2. Copying our design or creating one of your own, make separate pattern pieces for each section of appliqué. Cut all appliqué sections

47. Directions for making this laundry bag with jack-in-the-box appliqué are on pages 104-6. *(Photograph by O. Philip Roedel.)*

from fabrics and batting. (If appliqué is to be hand-sewn, allow ¼″ seam allowances on all fabrics but not on battings.)

3. Match battings and fabrics; pin and baste sections in place on front of bag and attach with a close zigzag stitch through one layer of bag only. (For hand-sewn, or blind appliqué: Turn under raw edges ¼″, pin sections in place on top of pillow case, and sew edges through all layers with small stitches.)

4. Open up top fold on bag. Along side fold make a faced slit 5½″ long. Fold bag fabric wrong side out; match and stitch across bottom and up side seam to within 5½″ of top edge. Finger press raw edge at top of bag under ½″, and selvages at side opening to inside. Stitch seam allowances along opening.

5. Turn hem inside (2½″), and make two rows of stitching to form casing. Insert cable cord through each casing and make a loop at each end for hanging.

Lessons in Inlay Work

Select designs for inlaid appliqué which do not depend on a variety of coloring for their attraction. Simple outlines are best, as intricate twists and turns are difficult to cut out and the finished work is apt to look ragged. A design suitable for a beginner is shown.

Table runner:

Materials needed are: 1½″ yards of natural-colored linen or fine crash 18 inches wide, one-half yard of the orange color in the same width, and two skeins each of stranded cotton in orange and bright green.

The runner should be just under 54 inches long, and between 13 and 18 inches wide, according to requirements.

Cut the orange linen in half, and line the two ends of the runner only, by cutting it one-half inch less in width, so that the ends of the natural-colored linen can be neatly turned over its raw edges. The edges of the runner should be all turned in and tacked down.

Build up your design from the pieces given in Fig. 18, trace onto the natural linen with carbon paper, placing it so that the outside point of the design is at least 1½ inches in from the edge of the runner at all points, though more plain linen can be allowed if desired.

To work the inlay, with the point of a very sharp pair of scissors, poke a hole through one of the leaves, piercing the natural linen only. Now cut away the natural linen inside the outline of the leaf. Before cutting away any more of the design, roughly overcast the natural-hued outlines to the orange material which is revealed beneath. This overcasting can be quite widely spaced, but it is a necessary precaution as the linen edges may begin to fray before the embroidery is begun.

The embroidery itself is done in close buttonhole stitch, keeping the purl edge along the cut outline, and making the stitches the depth of the double lines on the design.

When cutting out a flower, pin or tack down the center which is to remain, and cut away around the outer edge of the center.

Overcast both flower outline and center before beginning to embroider, and work the center with the buttonhole stitch to the outside. This can then be filled in with French knots or satin stitch (the latter not being quite so dainty in appearance as the knots). The flowers and centers are, of course, buttonholed with the orange cotton, and three threads in the needle are sufficient for the work throughout.

The turned-in and tacked edges of the runner can be machine hemstitched in either orange or green; or they can be given a buttonhole border, either in one of the colors, or a combination to the two—for example, green buttonhole stitches one-half inch in height and one-half inch apart, between which are orange buttonhole stitches, one-half inch in height.

Take out all tacking threads and press the work on the wrong side over a thick ironing blanket. The rest of the runner should be pressed with a damp cloth, if necessary, to remove creases.

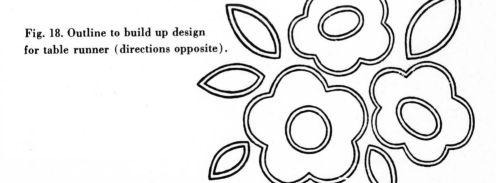

Fig. 18. Outline to build up design for table runner (directions opposite).

⑥ *Modern Appliqué*

Perhaps more than any other type of needlework, appliqué reflects the tremendous changes that have taken place in art and fashion. Since it is not restricted to the use of embroidery, it can be worked at a slow or fast tempo, an important consideration in a time-conscious age. Its practitioners can mix media, selecting such unconventional onlays as peach pits, glass chips, and paper straws. Appliqué work today is more than a vogue. It has attracted many artists who practice it as an art form, and it is taught as such in many art schools in the United States.

Non-Needlecraft Additions, A New Trend

Abstract expressionism, Op Art, Pop Art, junk culture, surrealism—all of these ideas have had widespread influence on craftsmen in every field. In needlework, totally different styles have emerged, products of the talented hands of designers concerned with aesthetic freedom. One has only to compare the laid-on materials used today with those of traditional appliqué to realize how far we have moved towards new visual "experiences" in an ancient craft.

What shall we call these new experiences? Are they "assemblages," "constructional appliqués," "dimensional appliqués," "fabric col-

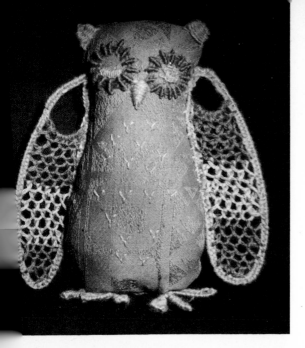

48. *(Left)* This stuffed appliqué owl is made from heavy linen embroidered in wool. Its wings are worked in buttonhole over wire and the feet are worked in cretan over wire before each is appliquéd to the body. *Bucky King.*

49. *(Below)* A turn-of-the-century embroidery by Jessie R. Newberry, one of the pioneers of modern work who introduced freer and more experimental techniques. This cushion cover is linen appliqué and silk embroidery on linen with satin stitch and borders of needleweaving. The flowers are pink; leaves and stems are two shades of green. *Victoria and Albert Museum.*

50. Man's first appliqué was of "found objects," probably stones, shells, and bones. Thus, "Seeds Growing" — with its beads, shells, cork, dried seed pods, and peach stones appliquéd with surface stitchery to heavy beige silk — is really a new interpretation of an old idea. *Bucky King.*

lages"? We shall have to develop an appropriate vocabulary for these forms (they are often misnamed "collage," which is generally meant as a collection of *flat* objects, and in modern needlework the added objects are often far from flat). Are they abstractions, representational pictures, interpretations?

Whatever we call them, these new embroideries include such non-needlework materials as peach pits (Plate 50), dried stems, weeds,

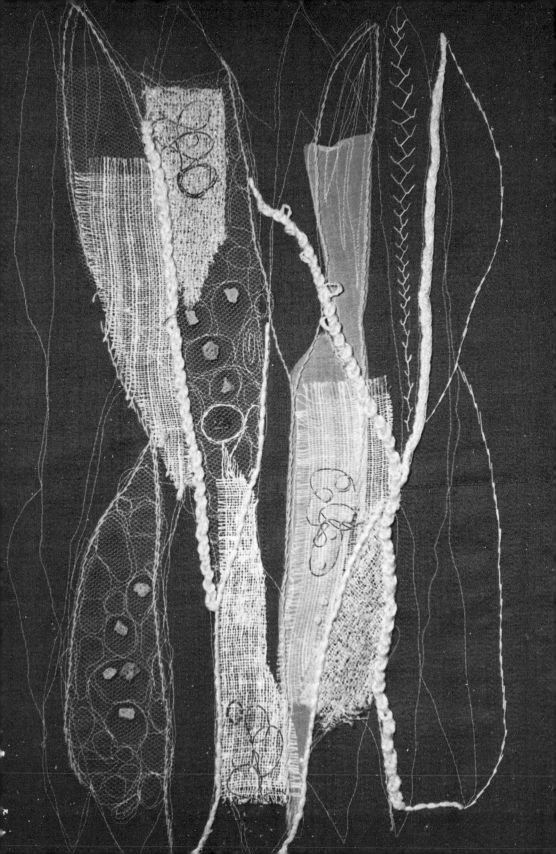

51. *(Opposite)* Designers treat art principles with respect, but man-made rules are meant to be broken. Here is a creative response to the injunction "do not use materials which fray." Designed and worked by Bucky King, "Cell Structure" is an appliqué of linen, organdy, and net using direct onlay method. Field stones and copper wire used in sections with both free machine embroidery and hand stitchery.

52. The term "collage" is appropriate for "Bull and Pigeons" because it is composed of flat fabrics. The wool background has appliqués of wool, satin, corduroy, velveteen, rayon, and lamé which are embroidered in silk, wool, fancy yarns, and metal threads using a variety of stitches including French knots, running stitches, and couching. *Margaret Kaye, Victoria and Albert Museum.*

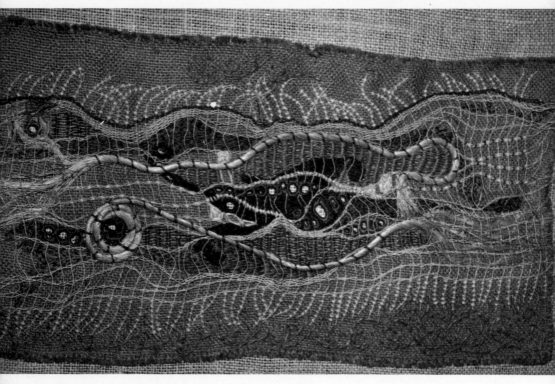

53. "To Peel an Onion" uses a plastic mesh onion bag, hemp rope, seeds, and linen fabrics in onlay appliqué techniques. *Nell Hall.*

54. *(Opposite)* "Noon," an appliqué and stitchery panel, uses white, yellow, and red transparent silks stitched to an ochre cotton ground with a variety of yarns, including mohair. *Nik Krevitsky.*

seeds, pods, cones, nuts, shells, miniature driftwood, skeletonized leaves and other "found objects." To make our designs even more *sui generis,* why not create mobiles and stabiles and other embroideries with units that seem to float in space? Can we activate units of needlework by combining detached appliqué methods with invisible nylon threads such as fishermen use? Good solutions to these and other technical problem will come as we continue to experiment and exercise our creative faculty.

This brings up a relevant point. Contemporary needleworkers share with other moderns the belief that mood and subject, rather than form

55. Bird Lady" has felt face and hands and wears a hat of straw over velvet. Her dress is adorned with beads, buttons, ball fringe, bias tape, ribbon, cotton yarn, and embroidery thread. Her stockings are black-striped cotton with leather shoes glued over them. Sophisticated and modern in use of materials, its story-telling quality is ageless in its appeal. *Shirley Kallus.*

and execution, are the essence of creativity. As a result, many pieces of stitchery seem crude and unfinished, brilliant in conception but haphazard in execution. Perhaps it is time for the truly creative talents which abound in our craft to set the pace for a disciplined approach to needlework and stitchery, a blending of the best of the old with the most exciting of the new.

Techniques with New Materials

Modern needleworkers have learned to exploit the potentials of color, texture, shape and line which exist in everyday objects. Cones, pods, seeds, nuts, produce from garden and pantry — to the seeing eye of the creative worker they are as useful in appliqué as are pieces of fabric or needle and thread. All this adds up to a need to develop special techniques for handling such a diversity of materials.

Nuts

Bore a hole through each one using a red-hot needle or nail held with padding. Fasten nut to background by pulling a wire or thread through the hole. Walnut shells can be opened and scraped clean inside. Pierce a hole at the edge as above. The shell may be shellacked with colorless nail polish for added luster. Pine cones can be cut in half and threads can be wrapped around their whorls, then stitched into place on the fabric.

Seeds

Washed seeds of all types can be sewn onto most fabrics while they are still slightly damp, when the needle can pierce them easily. They may also be pierced with a fine strong wire and threaded on the fabric. Discard any seeds which break in half. Seeds of sunflower, grapefruit, apple, melon, etc. are a few of the possibilities. Flat seeds such as sunflower may be used in the same manner as sequins, letting one overlap the other. Pine cones and composite seed structures may be separated into individual parts (or petals) and pierced with a needle, file or other sharp instrument for appliqué effects.

Peach pits

All peach pits and seeds which have internal seed structure or kernels must first have the kernel or internal seed removed. Slice the seed carefully in half if, like the peach pit, it does not separate of its own nature, and remove the kernel. Then drill the seed with a small hole or punch with a sharp pointed instrument such as a needle file.

7 Embroidery Stitches

Embroidery looks best when it is executed directly onto the ground fabric, but in appliqué work it is often used on the applied material as well, to fill in details, as in veins of leaves, features in animals, birds and human figures, and for other decorative purposes. It is also possible to work embroidery stitches continuously from the appliqué extending into the background fabric. This is a good device for bringing continuity to the design, since surface stitchery becomes the transitional or harmonizing element.

In the pages which follow you will find illustrated many stitches which are suited to appliqué, but they are for your general guidance only. The scope of stitchery is wide, and all the possibilities cannot be explored here.

Running Stitch

This is the simplest of all embroidery stitches, but for best effect care must be taken to keep every stitch of equal length. Bring thread through at right-hand end of line and work along the line, picking up a small piece of material at equal intervals. The length of the stitch and the piece picked up between can be varied as desired.

Overcast

Back Stitch

Starting ⅛ inch from right-hand end, take thread down at extreme right-hand end and bring it up ¼ inch farther along; then for second stitch take it down where the thread first came up. This completes two stitches. Continue in same way, picking up ¼ inch each time; or stitches can be made any length desired.

When a close raised line is required, this is the best stitch to use. Work over one or more strands of the same thread as will be used for the overcasting, bringing the thread through the material at the beginning of the line and holding it down over the line. Then stitch over the laid thread or threads, picking up each time a very small piece of material as the diagram shows. The top stitches must go straight across the line, therefore the needle slants slightly at each new stitch so that the thread is brought up in position for the next stitch.

Stem Stitch

Start at end of line and work from left to right, inserting needle from right to left; advance the length required for the stitch and pick up material slightly less than half the length of the stitch, keeping the thread below the needle. In subsequent stitches the needle should be brought up just above the end of the previous stitch. For a thick stem-stitch make each new stitch advance half the length of the previous one by bringing the needle out at the top of the previous stitch; back stitch will then result on the reverse side.

Lazy Daisy Stitch

One of the most popular of stitches, and, as its name implies, the easiest way to make a daisy petal. Bring thread through at the base of a petal, hold it down under the left thumb, insert needle where thread first came through and bring it up again just inside petal tip and over the held thread, then draw the thread through and take it to the back again outside the loop, so keeping the loop in place.

Chain Stitch

Chain is one of the most popular of embroidery stitches, is quickly effective, and goes smoothly along any straight or curved line. Starting at the right-hand end, bring the thread through the material, then, holding it down in a loop under the left thumb, pass the needle down exactly where the thread came through, and up a small distance along the line, within the loop held by the thumb ; draw the thread through, so forming a loop with the thread coming out within its base. Repeat in the same way for each stitch. To finish a line take the thread to the back just beyond the loop of the last chain.

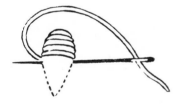

Satin Stitch (1)

One of the most popular of 'solid' stitches, satin-stitch is useful for filling practically any not-too-wide shape. The stitches are just worked over and over the space, the needle coming up on one edge and going down on the opposite edge. Care must be taken to keep all stitches parallel and close together, as it is essential for good effect that the work is perfectly even . . . . that it has in fact a satin smooth finish.

Satin Stitch (2)

When the shape to be embroidered has a centre " vein", work as for Satin Stitch above, but slant the stitches and work in two sections meeting down centre.

Zigzag Chain

This is worked in the same way as Chain Stitch, but for each chain the needle is taken diagonally across the line of working, first in one direction, then in the other.

Zigzag Chain Variation

Similar in effect to the **Zigzag Chain**, in this variation each chain is held down at its tip with a separate stitch as when working Lazy Daisy Stitch (page 120). Make the first chain as described for Chain Stitch but diagonally across the line to be covered, then take the needle down over the loop of the chain and up again within the loop, ready to work the next chain. Repeat this all along.

Padded Satin Stitch (1)

When a raised effect is required, first pad the shape with stitches then Satin Stitch over the padding. Various padding stitches can be used. Above, the shape is padded with straight stitches worked lengthways, and the satin stitch is worked over them in a slanting direction. This is particularly good for leaf shapes.

Padded Satin Stitch (2)

To keep a satin stitch spot a good round, work the padding by satin stitching in one direction, keeping the stitches just within the outline, then satin stitch over it in the opposite direction.

Padded Satin Stitch (3)

This is an excellent way to pad a satin stitch line ; first work a row of Chain Stitch (page 3) along the line, using sufficient number of strands nearly to fill the required width, then satin stitch over it at right angles to the chain stitch.

Padded Satin Stitch (4)

Another way of getting a raised effect, especially on narrow leaf shapes, is to work two layers of Satin Stitch, the first one slanting in one direction, the second in the opposite direction.

Open Buttonhole

Probably one of the most widely used embroidery stitches, this form of buttonhole stitch is not only useful for edging a shape, but the upright spokes give a quickly achieved decorative effect. Bring the needle out on the lower line, hold thread under left thumb, take needle down on upper line and bring it out on lower line immediately below ; draw thread through, passing needle over the held down thread. Work in this way throughout, spacing stitches as required.

Long and Short Stitch

This is the most useful and most widely used stitch for shaded flower embroidery, as the stitches of one row, being long and short, dovetail into those in the subsequent row, giving a gradual merging of colouring. The general direction of the stitches, when worked on flower-petal or leaf, should be towards the heart cf the flower, or the vein or base of a leaf, following the natural grain of the real flower subject. Start with a row of stitches along the edge of the shape to be filled, making the top of the stitches on the outline and the other ends long and short alternately; then fill in, row by row, till the base or vein is reached, changing colour or shade as required. The sketch below shows the second row of stitching in operation.

Laid Stitch

Suitable for filling large spaces with smooth stitchery, using stranded or floss-type silks or crewel wools. Take a succession of stitches across space from side to side, picking up sufficient on edge to allow for width of another stitch (as needle in diagram); fill in with a second set of stitches (dark in diagram for clarity) between the first.

Satin Stitch Appliqué

Cut material exact size of shape to be covered, and tack to background by lightly overcasting raw edges. Satin Stitch evenly over edge of appliqué, taking each stitch into the ground below.

Flower in Pin
Stitch Appli-
qué. Stamens
French Knots.

Pin Stitch Appliqué

Cut out shape to be applied, lightly tack
in place, and Pin Stitch as diagrams 1, 2, 3, 4,
turning in edges with the point of the needle
as the work proceeds. Use a single strand of
fine cotton and a large needle. If very
defined holes are required, work with a
punch needle, tying the end of the thread
into the eye so that it will not pull out whilst
working.

1. Bring thread
through from
back of work to
right side, just
above the turned-
in edge of
material to be
applied, and pick
up small piece of
the ground just
below appliqué.

1

2. Stitch again
over the same
piece of the
ground material,
using the same
holes as made
here by the pre-
vious stitch.

3. Again using same hole as
made by the meeting of the
first stitches, take the needle
behind the work diagonally to
bring thread into same position
as 1, ready to work next stitch.

4. Here is the
effect obtained
when steps 1, 2
and 3 are re-
peated continu-
ously. The defined
holes are formed
by drawing the
stitches tightly.

4

Hemmed Appliqué

Cut shape to be applied ⅛ inch larger than
design to be covered, and lightly tack in
position, then, turning in the ⅛ inch with
point of needle as the work proceeds, hem in
place as diagram shows, making the stitches
as invisible as possible.

Buttonhole Appliqué

A good stitch for edging appliqué as it can
be worked over the raw edges of the applied
material. Tack the cut-out shape on the
foundation material, then work buttonhole
stitch over the edge of the cut-out through
both materials, keeping the stitches fairly
short and close together.

Bibliography

BAXTER, NANCY. *Needlecraft for Home Decoration.* New York: Hearthside, 1966.

CAVE, OENONE. *Linen Cut-work.* New York: Hearthside, 1963.

CHRISTIE, MRS. ARCHIBALD. *Samplers and Stitches.* London: Batsford, 1959.

FREEHOF, LILLIAN S., and KING, BUCKY. *Embroideries and Fabrics for Synagogue and Home.* New York: Hearthside, 1966.

HINSON, DOLORES A. *Quilting Manual.* New York: Hearthside, 1966.

KING, BUCKY. *Creative Canvas Embroidery.* New York: Hearthside, 1963.

MORRIS, BARBARA J. *History of English Embroidery.* London: Victoria and Albert Museum, 1951.

Notes on Applied Work and Patchwork. London: Victoria and Albert Museum, 1938.

SNOOK, BARBARA. *Learning to Embroider.* New York: Hearthside, 1963.

Index